THE COMPETITIVE EDGE

THE COMPETITIVE EDGE

Improving Your Dressage Scores
in the Lower Levels
Revised Edition

BY MAX GAHWYLER
CARTOONS BY PATRICIA PEYMAN NAEGELI

Half Halt Press
Boonsboro, Maryland

**The Competitive Edge: Improving Your Dressage
Scores in the Lower Levels,** *Revised Edition*
This revised edition © 1995 Half Halt Press
© 1989 Half Halt Press
Previous revised edition © 1990 Half Halt Press

Published in the United States of America by
Half Halt Press, Inc.
P.O. Box 67
Boonsboro, MD 21713

Cartoons by Patricia Peyman Naegeli, after doodles by the author.

AHSA tests and excerpts from tests reproduced with the kind permission of
The American Horse Shows Association, Inc.

Library of Congress Cataloging-in-Publication Data

Gahwyler, Max, 1923-
    The competitive edge: Improving your dressage scores in the lower / by
Max Gahwyler: cartoons by Patricia Peyman Naegeli.--
Rev. ed.
        p. cm.
    ISBN 0-939481-43-x
    1. Dressage--Competitions. 2. Dressage test. I. Title.
SF309.6.G34 1995
798.2'4 dc20

                                                        95-20098
                                                        CIP

CONTENTS

INTRODUCTION

I N no other sport but dressage does everybody compete together. Olympic caliber riders present their young horses in the same classes as Pony Clubbers. True amateurs with their pet horses, able only to ride an hour in the evening and on weekends, show against what we might call "professional" amateurs, who are able to afford continuous coaching, the best horses and have an unlimited amount of time and money. And, there are also the true professionals, for whom showing is a marketing activity.

This book is addressed to the true amateur who is trying to work his or her way into this sport and hopes to be reasonably successful. The rider who has been showing successfully in the higher levels has probably developed his own system and, consciously or unconsciously, avoids the mistakes that ruin so many otherwise good rides. It is often distressing to me as a judge to be forced to mark down a performance because of easily avoidable mistakes that are unrelated to riding ability, training or potential of the horse. I frequently see a professional or advanced amateur win on a less well-trained horse simply because of show ring experience and smart planning of the ride.

The thoughts and reflections in this book were written while traveling to and from shows, waiting for airplane connections and rides to the show ground, waiting between rides at competitions and all the other waiting in a judge's career. It reflects my firm conviction that most riders could do much better if only they would think through the problem ahead. I hope this book will help the beginner and amateur rider to shorten his or her apprenticeship in this exacting and intellectual sport by pointing out some simple ways to make showing more fun and more successful.

Please note that this is not intended as a training manual; there are many excellent texts available as well as fine instructors. It is intended to help refine competition technique for the amateur or beginning rider.

I dedicate this book to them.

Darien, Connecticut

CHAPTER ONE:

CLASSICAL DRESSAGE & MODERN COMPETITION

MODERN competitive dressage riding in its present form is, historically speaking, a rather recent equestrian endeavor. The concept is new in comparison to the centuries of horsemanship before us and it behooves us to understand its relationship to the past as well as what we are doing differently today.

The origin of present day concepts of training the horse can arbitrary be fixed to the time of the court of Naples, when Pignatelli and Grisone published their first manuscript on horse training in 1532. This began a continuous stream of writing on horses, including the publications of Pluvinelle in 1623, Newcastle in 1645, de la Gueriniere in 1729, Seeger in 1834, Oyenhauser in 1848, Steinbrecht in 1895, and the authors of the last 50 years: Seunig, Podhajsky; Watjen, Museler, Decarpentry, etc.

Later publishers and authors of this century have interpreted these original teachings and adapted them to a modern type of riding, taking into account the changes in types of horses that have evolved over the years.

It is noteworthy that the principles of de la Gueriniere became the basis of the Spanish Riding School in Vienna where we can still see classical riding as it has been practiced after three centuries of development. Since we no longer ride many of the movements of classical dressage, we can only hope that they will be preserved in this living museum for many generations to come.

Where is the common denominator between the past and present? It lies in the basic training of the horse, up to about our Third or Fourth Level, where the horse learns to move forward, to be straight, supple, balanced, light in front, and on the bit. The methods we use to achieve this—shoulder-in, travers, renvers, simple changes, half-passes, smaller and smaller circles, circles on two-tracks, rein backs, and so on—are nothing more than schooling exercises and were called the Campaign school. These exercises originate directly from the classical training of the young horse as expounded by the Old Masters, and enabled the horse to become sufficiently athletic to reach the highest level of the haute ecole. It is these movements and methods of training that have been incorporated into our national tests from Training through Fourth Level.

Where we begin to see a significant difference from classical haute ecole is in the FEI levels. Classical dressage was subdivided into the "airs above the ground" movements such as croupade, ballotade, capriole and courbette, and the movements on the ground such as the mezair, levade, passage, piaffe, pirouette, passade, redop, and work between the pillars (more of a training exercise than an end movement in itself). In all of these movements, the emphasis was always on collection and execution of the individual movements, done to perfection, rather than a sequence of movements as in the modern day dressage test.

Flying changes every stride were added to the classical movements by Baucher between 1820 and 1830. This new movement was received with an outcry of indignation at the time as a "circus trick" that taught the horse to pace at the canter. It was ultimately accepted, however, by even the Spanish Riding School because of its spectacular aspects and the difficulty in riding it correctly. Of all the elements of classical dressage, only a few are found in modern dressage tests: piaffe, passage, pirouette, one-tempe changes, two-track work in either zig-zag or on a steep angle as in the half-pass. These last two movements are extensions of the original basic training. Everything else has been dropped and is not required or performed in the dressage tests of today.

What is most different in modern competitive dressage from the classical concepts is the uninterrupted flow of movement after movement in a fixed, prescribed test. There are no breaks or

arbitrary selections of where movements are to be executed, even if the horse is ill-prepared.

This continuity from movement to movement by necessity introduced the riding of transitions, since movements were no longer ridden for and by themselves but became an integral part of a continuous, flowing exercise. The first elements in the development in this modern direction were apparent at the beginning of the twentieth century when the concept of the modern dressage test was incorporated in the 1912 Olympic Games.

Since the manege where classical riding was performed was usually a rather small courtyard, the concept of medium or extended gaits in classical exercises did not exist and could not have been executed within the physical confines of the training facilities of the day. In addition, the Renaissance or Baroque horse such as the Lipizzaner is not built for the gaits as we see them today.

In the 1920's, the notion of a large standard arena with fixed points was introduced, bringing with it the concept of absolute precision as well as enough space to demand anything from extended to collected gaits. No one seems to know for certain the rationale behind the selection and location of the letters.

These two elements together—movement after movement and the fixed arena of precise dimensions—created the basis for the modern dressage test. We have elevated the basic schooling exercises of the Classical period, developed for the training of any good horse, to the dressage requirements of the National levels while eliminating most of the classical movements from FEI competition requirements. With the introduction of a standard rectangle arena, and the concept of gaits, transitions, and a continuous flow of movement, twentieth century competitive dressage was created.

But the common bond with the past remains in the correct basic training of the horse. The basic concepts and proven training methods of the Old Masters remain the cornerstone for correct schooling of any young horse, irrespective of the ultimate use we make of the horse.

Heaven for
Dressage Horses

A: What did you do best?
B: Caprioles, balotades courbettes, and you?
A: Gaits and transitions.
B: What are those? Are you sure you
were a Dressage horse?
A: Never heard of your stuff either!
B: Let's compare notes.

There can be no short cuts or deviations from the basic classical training methods and concepts. If short cuts are attempted, horse and rider will pay a stiff penalty when trying to move to the higher levels. Without the basic classical training, modern competitive dressage riding is not possible, irrespective of how far removed it is from the haute ecole of the Old Masters.

CHAPTER TWO:

THE BASICS OF DRESSAGE COMPETITION

DRESSAGE competition should be some fun, particularly in the lower levels. You are perfectly entitled to smile at the mishaps of your competitors if you can just as easily laugh at yourself and your own misfortunes. Put in perspective, all you have to do is induce your horse to show his best side for five minutes in front of the judge. For all the feed, grooming, tidbits, and care provided, this appears to be a small favor to ask of your four-legged friend but it is not horse logic.

But if you really understand the basics of the sport, the horse you are riding, the elements of judging, and what you are supposed to do in the ring, things will begin to fall in place for you.

The basic difference that I see between a professional and amateur is that the professional really rides every step of the test, practically carrying his horse on a silver platter through the movement. He is supportive like a nursemaid supporting the first step of an infant. He never puts his horse in a position the horse cannot handle confidently. On the other hand, the beginner or amateur frequently expects the horse to do everything, and often

has a confused idea of what is actually expected of him. He tends to put his horse in difficult situations, expecting the impossible, such as a blue ribbon for his horse's valiant efforts.

Let's remember, failure to do well is always the rider's fault, winning is the accomplishment of the horse.

Scoring makes sense only when competitor and judge are knowledgeable of the basic rules governing the performance. And this is where the American Horse Shows Association (AHSA) comes in with rules, regulations, standards, descriptions and definitions of movements which every judge has to know and follow. But while the AHSA requires judges to know this, no one has any power over competitors.

Nevertheless, in order to make sense, both parties, the one behind and the one in front of C, must know the guidelines of the sport equally well to avoid misunderstandings and disappointments. Agreeing or disagreeing with the present AHSA definitions is beside the point; every judge has to score according to those established guidelines, and not according to his personal opinion.

But what about the competitor? Has he or she (or their instructor) ever read the ASHA definition of the levels, tests, and movements to be shown? From what I have seen, only a very few riders have done so. In order to plan the ride and later understand the comments, suggestions, and scores of the judge, the rider must have a basic understanding of the criteria by which he and his horse are being evaluated. Every dressage competitor must have a current ASHA *Rule Book* and have read very carefully the sections concerning the level at which he is showing. It becomes quite evident that many of the top professionals know these rules very well while most of the amateurs simply do not. So take the time to read the *Rule Book* and understand clearly what will be expected of you at each level.

DEFINITIONS OF THE LEVELS

The progression from Training to Second Level should reflect the increasing balance, straightness, and suppleness of the horse, the ability to master more and more demanding transitions, and demonstrate true dressage gaits, acceptance of the bit and forwardness

It is only in Second Level that some of the basic tools for achieving engagement, collection, and medium gaits are intro-

duced. These tools are basically the same as the classical training tools used by the Old Masters to achieve increasing straightness, suppleness, and self-carriage of the horse.

Third Level introduces the basic lateral movements. At Fourth Level, Prix St. Georges, and Intermediare I, there are not as many new movements introduced as there are refinements of movements already learned from Second and Third Levels. The transitions are more difficult because there is less time for preparation.

The next big step is Intermediare II and Grand Prix. Movements from the classical haute ecole of dressage are incorporated as an integral part of the test. These movements include the passage, piaffe, pirouette, and single-tempe changes. The difficulty of the test is determined by the sequence of movements and transitions, as well as the quality of gaits required for their proper execution.

The 1995 tests, to my mind, are much less open to misunderstanding than the previous ones. Guidelines were established with the input of over 20 of the most distinguished U.S. dressage riders which helped correctly focus the tests.

As a result, the tests are progressively demanding with the main emphasis on forwardness (leading to impulsion), acceptance of the bit (leading to being "on the bit" and the aids), emphasis on equal suppleness (straightness), and correct transitions, based on a harmonious development of horse and rider.

But let's go back to the basics and the beginning of every Grand Prix horse, the Training Level.

TRAINING LEVEL

"Purpose: To confirm that the horse's muscles are supple, loose, and it moves forward in a clear and steady rhythm, accepting contact with the bit."

– AHSA Definition

In this current definition, acceptance of the bit, perhaps the most misunderstood concept in the 1991 tests, has been replaced by a description of what it really is. Too many inexperienced riders and instructors understood this as pulling the front of the horse into an artificial frame. This was too often done by creating pain, with sharp bits and, if that did not work, with draw reins and hand riding. This is not dressage.

Acceptance of contact with the bit requires very steady hands, no seesawing, and a horse finding his balance. The rider determines the frame, the horse determines the pressure in his mouth, and riding a horse at this stage is basically lungeing the horse from the saddle. The hands should be nothing more but a soft and steady attachment of well adjusted reins.

At this level, what we do not yet expect is engagement, collection, or impulsion. We do expect, however, the basic requirements for any dressage horse: a degree of straightness, the ability to execute transitions, and a certain quality of gait. This is amply highlighted in the directive ideas. In addition, many scores in the Training Level tests are located for transitions only.

Riding at Training Level requires a very tactful rider with total balance in the saddle and an understanding of the aids. Unfortunately, this is a combination seen only rarely. If there is a very experienced rider in your class, take the opportunity to watch him ride the test; you can learn a lot on what to do and what not to do. Suddenly, even a Training Level test can become fluid, forward, balanced, rhythmic, and a pleasure to watch (and to score by the judge).

It is in the Training Level that the conformation of the horse varies the most depending on the breed, as every good judge knows. The horses' basic way of going varies enormously. Just compare a young Thoroughbred to a young European Warmblood. Thoroughbreds tend to be long, lanky, and way out in front of the vertical. The European Warmbloods tend to carry themselves in a certain frame, with an arched neck, high poll and close to a vertical head position. With the current definition, the Thoroughbred must learn to accept the contact and therefore a

certain frame before you show him. This obviously requires more time, equestrian skill and effort than for a Warmblood–or Andalusians and Lusitanos!

Unfortunately, some competitors buy very advanced horses, then drop them down into Training Level, which is obvious to any experienced observer. I consider this practice to be unfair to the other competitors, and one that should not rate very high with judges

These horses simply carry themselves and their inexperienced rider in a manner which is not consistent with Training Level, and should be scored accordingly.

If you are showing a horse in this category, I suggest starting him at First or Second Level, where his qualities will better fit the definitions of the test. But, after a while, even these horses regress to the level of their riders. No horse stays better than the rider on his back for very long.

FIRST LEVEL

"Purpose: To confirm that the horse, in addition to the requirements of Training Level, has developed thrust (pushing power) and achieved a degree of balance and throughness.

– AHSA Definition

Basically, this is simply a continuation and development of Training Level goals. The fact that you can ride the First Level patterns is not the deciding factor, but the concept of quality. Be certain to read the directive ideas on the AHSA test sheet for each First Level test.

Let's look at the similarities between Training and First Level. These include forward movement, regularity of rhythm, riding straight lines, riding circles, and turns in the walk, trot, and canter, transitions at the letters, and the acceptance of the correct aids, including the bit.

What has been added in First Level?

■ Thrust: what does that mean? It means you cannot just get some sort of frame with the horse in front, accepting the bit. The horse must be ridden from behind, into the bit, and not just held in front. This is the absolute basis of First Level. Without the thrust from behind, no real dressage is possible, and it is made very clear that the foundation of future work has to be accomplished here in First Level. So, don't just be concerned about shortening the frame and keeping the horse on the bit, but be sure the horses haunches are very active, pushing and progressively increasing the action of the hocks.

■ Trot transitions in and out of the halt with no walk allowed.

■ Straightness is more important and, if not completed, should at least be attempted.

■ Lateral suppleness is asked for in smaller circles (10 meters at the trot and 15 meters in the canter) , and must be equal on both sides.

■ Longitudinal suppleness must be shown by a lengthening of the stride, or by a free walk with the horse stretching into longer reins. The rider should be able to bring the horse back into the medium walk with easy acceptance of the bit. In the transitions, there should be no resistance shown, and rhythm and regularity should remain constant. The horse has not learned to accept the bit correctly if he resists these demands.

Concerning lengthening, note that the directive ideas indicate that the transitions into and out of movements, as well as the quality of the gait in which the movement is shown, are more important than the degree of lengthening of the stride. Why is this? Because unless the transitions are learned correctly, there is no chance of developing correct medium gaits, and progressing on to Second Level. Lengthening of the stride does not mean barreling across the diagonal or down the long side on a running horse at full speed.

Note that acceptance of the bit is not a matter of pulling the head of the horse; rather, it marks the beginning of some engagement and self-carriage. This allows the horse to become more elevated in the neck, shorter in the body, and lighter on the forehand. There should be no leaning on the bit, or pulling, and no heaviness on the forehand.

The horse should accept these demands when asked by the rider's seat and leg aids without any resistance. A key transition in First Level tests occurs after the walk on the long rein. Here, the horse should return to a shorter frame while accepting the bit, showing no signs of resistance, change of rhythm, or length of stride.

The beginning of self-carriage becomes visible in the transitions from trot to canter and canter to trot. If the transition is not executed from the haunches, the canter depart results in the horse being heavy on his forehand.

The canter departs must be made precisely at the letter. The inside hind leg should come under the horse, and the subsequent canter on the long side should be ridden on a straight line, with the horse's forehand positioned slightly to the inside. For example, in First Level Test 1, falling into the canter in the corner with the haunches crooked (on the inside of the track) is considered insufficient at this level.

Why are judges so severe in their expectations of the executions of the transitions and movements at First Level? Why can't the horse just proceed in a Training Level frame and gaits, remaining heavy on the forehand through the transitions, and run or rush on the diagonal with or without any lengthening?

The reason is because First Level is an important step in the green, unbalanced horse's development, and serves as the preparation for the true dressage gaits in Second Level, the collected and medium gaits. Unless the basics at First Level are correct, the horse and rider will never perform properly at Second Level, and certainly not at any of the succeeding levels.

SECOND LEVEL

"Purpose: To confirm that the horse, having demonstrated that it has achieved the thrust (pushing power) required in First Level, now shows that through additional training it accepts more weight on the hind quarters (collection), shows the thrust required at medium paces and is reliably on the bit. Greater degree of straightness, bending, suppleness, throughness and self-carriage is required than at First Level.

– AHSA Definition

There is no question that true dressage begins at Second Level. There are no more working gaits as in the past. From Second Level Test 1 on, there is collected trot and canter. Unless your First Level work has been impeccable, and unless you have the correct gaits, riding just the patterns of the tests will not be sufficient.

The basic difference between the working gaits required in Training and First Level and the collected and medium gaits required later is not, as many think, in the shortening or lengthening of the stride, but in impulsion and engagement. Impulsion supplies the drive to move freely forward from behind, with the front end being more elevated with self-carriage due to adequate engagement. The horse is light and consistent on the bit under all circumstances. The working gaits lack this degree of impulsion.

Again, the movements and transitions asked for in Second Level— trot/canter/trot transitions, walk/canter departs, shoulder-in, travers, medium trot, and the simple changes—are really just the teaching exercises from the classical school used to develop impulsion, engagement, and acceptance of the bit and aids. The Second Level tests demonstrate to the judge your ability to begin to use the tools of the classical masters correctly and successfully.

The Logic of Training through Second Level

So we see that there is a logical progression from Training to Second Level, one that increasingly tests the green horse' s development and points the way to the development of his full athletic potential.

Remember, it is usually more difficult to teach a horse to go on the bit, showing impulsion, engagement and self-carriage, than it is to teach piaffe to a horse who has learned the basics correctly.

That is why there are absolutely no short cuts at this stage of training. Faulty basic training will become evident at Second, Third, or Fourth Level, with no advancement possible. It is much better to spend the time needed at the lower levels, thus enabling the horse to progress more easily and steadily later.

Now it may seem unfortunate that the difficulties of training a horse are more concentrated at the beginning than later on, since it is unavoidable to make mistakes unless we are highly

experienced trainers (and even they will admit to their share of mistakes!). But, remember, riding dressage is a life-long experience in learning and improving. Absolute perfection is impossible. Learn from your mistakes, and use the judge's comments on your test to improve your at-home schooling. Listen to good advice and read as much of the classical literature as you can lay your hands on.

Above all, don't blame your horse if you do not succeed. It is an old saying that the biggest handicap a horse has to live with is the level of competence of the rider on his back, which is always the limiting factor for not achieving his true athletic potential. If things don't work out, look at yourself and what you are doing. You must learn from your mistakes and advance your knowledge in order to improve.

As you improve, your horse will improve, and your test scores will improve. Once the movements and transitions at each level have been mastered, your scores will be consistently above 60 percent. You are then ready to move to the next higher level.

Modern competition dressage and the progression from level to level is based not so much on the difficulty of the movements themselves, but in the way they are arranged within the test. The key is in the more and more demanding transitions, and in the quality of the gaits in which the movements and transitions must be performed.

It is in the fluidity, balance, and rhythm leading to the ability to shift gaits and position instantly which is the true art of modern dressage riding.

These three basic element—transitions, quality of gait, and the movements—are the foundation of all lower level tests and the key to success.

The next three chapters will examine each element in detail.

CHAPTER THREE:

TRANSITIONS

TRANSITION is the single most frequently used word in any dressage test from Training Level to Grand Prix–and the most overlooked. Notice the use of transition under "Directive Ideas" on any test sheet; it is the underlying concept of both dressage performance and judging.

Another indication of the importance of transitions is given by the allocation of separate scores to key transitions on the test sheets instead of simply judging them as part of the greater movement. This starts as early as Training Level.

Every movement in a test has at least two transitions: one getting in and another to get out. If either of these transitions is not well done, the succeeding movement will be a problem. There will be no 8's on a test score unless both the movement and the related transitions are well-executed.

Transitions are also a key element in the progression of difficulty among the tests. For example, let's look at the canter requirements in the Training Level tests. In Training Level, the canter transition is made between two letters, from K and A for example, in a corner limited by the enclosure of the ring. There is no need for the horse to respond immediately to the aids, or to be straight or engaged. Instead, cantering on the correct lead—

sooner or later—when asked, is the major concern at this level.

At First Level, however, the transition into the canter is to be made at the letter; no option, no leeway. The trot and canter are the same as required in the earlier tests. It is the specificity of the exact location of where the transition is to be made that introduces, for the first time, the element of precision. This becomes a test of the responsiveness of the horse and the skill of the rider.

As another example of the progressively difficult demands in transitions, let's consider the halt at X, where the movement calls for a trot–halt–trot transition. In Training Level, the rider is allowed a few steps of walk through the transition. In First Level, however, this is not allowed and is rated "insufficient." Again, the trot and halt are the same as in Training Level, performed in the working gaits, but what a world of difference if one cannot take a few steps of walk anymore!

While initially all transitions to and from the canter are made through the trot, this changes in Second Level where the walk–canter and canter–walk transitions are introduced. No trot steps are allowed, and the sequence of transitions is concluded in the canter–walk–canter movement (the "simple change"). The canter or the walk is not the problem for most of us; the correct way to proceed from one to the other is.

In the subsequent chapter devoted to the movements, we will look at many more such examples, and consider the best ways to ride them. For now, though, remember that a dressage test is not simply a sequence of separate movements, but the harmonious flow from one exercise or gait to another in a progressively demanding fashion. The transitions determine, even at Training Level, the quality of the performance. The transitions preceding and following the movement contribute heavily to the score received. For this reason, the locations of the transitions have been changed in the 1995 tests from those in previous tests to be fair to the horse, but they are judged separately as to their proper execution. Anyone interested in winning should spend at least as much time and energy on perfecting transitions as on the movements themselves.

Why are the transitions so important? Riding transitions is carrying the fundamental elements of dressage from one movement or gait to another, such as rhythm, straightness, engagement, acceptance of the bit, lightness, cadence, and balance. Think about the mechanism of a natural transition of a young, untrained horse under saddle. In the up transition, the movement starts in the front, where the horse needs his neck and head to balance himself. If the rider does not give or have soft hands, the horse throws his head up, pulls on the reins, or uses the bit as a fifth leg until he finds his balance in a few strides.

In the down transition, the brakes are in front: the horse "falls on his forehand," leans on the bit, or fights the reins to gain freedom for his neck and head to regain his balance.

We want just the opposite, of course: all changes of gait, lengthening and slowing down, to come from behind. The front end of the horse should remain light, steady, and as raised as the level of training permits. It is only in this frame that it will be possible to maintain the quality of gaits, from one movement to another, and to allow for the development of more and more difficult movements.

How do we develop this ability? Very progressively, because the quality of the transitions is tied directly with the ability to use and engage the hindquarters. For this reason, on a young horse, the transitions are much easier on a circle than on a straight line, where at least the inside hind quarter is already engaged.

What is the "secret" of developing engagement, self-carriage, and transitions from behind? It is the half halt, the key foundation of any transition.

The half halt is executed by pivoting the seat bone forward and upward. Since, anatomically speaking, we have no muscles in the back to push our seat forward—irrespective of all the equestrian expressions used to define this change of seat such as "brace your back"—it is actually executed by the long abdominal muscles pulling the pelvis up. Sitting up and taking a deep breath puts you deeper into the saddle since the raised rib cage automatically pulls the seat forward and up, causing the rider to sit deeper on the seat bones. This movement, combined with leg pressure behind the girth, activates the horse's back and abdominal muscles, bringing the hind legs a little more under the horse, and making the hind legs carry more weight.

The second part of the half halt is the rider's hands. If we let go with them at the moment we change our seat, the horse stretches out, takes longer strides, and falls on the forehand. But, if at the same time we close our fingers with a slight tug, the rear end of the horse moves closer to the front. This results in a slightly higher and better self-carriage in front. This is where we want to be before, during, and after the transition. The key to successful half halts lies in the coordination of the aids and the instant relaxation once executed. Initially, it may have to be done several times in sequence, but eventually it becomes a conditioned reflex of the rider and a conditioned response of the horse.

While simple and crude at the beginning of the training of the horse, the half halt becomes, with time, the most subtle and effective communication between horse and rider.

So, the first step in learning correct transitions is to teach the horse to respond to simple, undemanding half halts. The quality of the transitions will improve as the horse begins to understand this, and becomes better able to respond physically to your aids.

A lot of lower level tests are won by upper level riders showing young horses because they know exactly how to ride soft and effective half halts. They know how to set the horse up and how to use this technique to keep the horse from falling off balance or onto the forehand when riding a change in direction or gait.

The ability to ride effective half halts is so essential for an active competitive rider that this cannot be emphasized enough. It is nothing glamorous; it is nothing to show off to your friends. It is practically invisible except to the experienced eye. But once half halts have been mastered, they will make a world of difference in your ability to get a horse properly in and out of a movement, and to regain balance and acceptance of the bit if lost.

Here are two practical examples of the correct use of half halts in transitions:

First, consider the canter depart from the trot in Training Level Test 1 and 2 with a horse that is not quite far enough along to be really on the bit. Nonetheless, the canter depart should be smooth, and allow the horse to use his neck and head for balancing. While approaching K for the canter depart, start the first half halt right after V, and repeat again a stride or two later. Be sure to use your seat equally, pushing into both hands, with an instant soft opening of the fingers afterwards. Upon reaching K, repeat the half halt, but release only the inside rein, while simultaneously giving the aids for the canter depart, using primarily the inside seat and leg. The horse will jump from behind into the soft inside rein, while the still-holding outside rein prevents the horse from rushing or from falling too much on the forehand. Once in the canter, the inside fingers give with every canter stride to allow the movement to go through the horse, while at the same time allowing him to balance himself.

A much more difficult transition is the simple change in Second Level. It can only be ridden properly on a horse that carries more weight on his hind legs, and has sufficiently shortened his stride in the canter to "march'"into a clean walk from behind. During the circular approach to the movement, we use our half halts for several canter strides, while staying soft but giving less on the inside rein. When the horse is sufficiently collected, the last half halt is ridden into both hands, while the driving aids of the rider stop. Once the horse obeys, we release a little bit, take 3 walk steps with a soft half halt into both hands, followed by a release on the new inside rein, coordinated with the aids for the canter depart. The key is the correct coordination between the holding and releasing on the new inside rein, and the driving aids, with your supporting half halt.

Looking at the lower level tests, we see three basic types of transitions:

1. Transitions between Gaits

■ Up transitions on a straight line or on a large circle from the halt to the walk, from the walk to the trot, and from the trot to the canter.

■ Down transitions on a straight line or on a large circle from the canter to the trot, from the trot to the walk, from the walk to the halt.

■ Transitions skipping one stage such as halt to trot, walk to canter, trot to halt, or canter to walk.

■ Transitions skipping two gaits in the sequence, such as halt to canter, canter to halt (which starts at Third Level).

2. Transitions within Gaits

■ Free walk to medium walk, up to collected walk to extended walk.
■ Working trot to lengthened trot and back to working trot. Same sequence for the canter.
■ Collected trot to medium trot or extended trot and back collected trot. Same sequence for the canter.

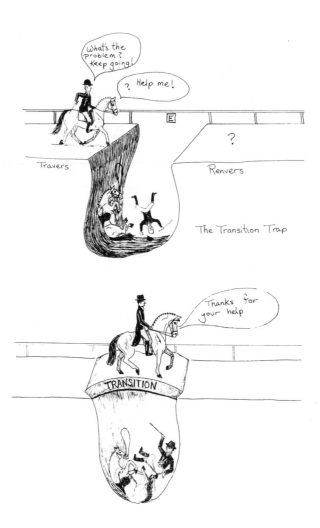

The Transition Trap

3. Lateral Transitions

■ Bending from left to right from a straight line.
■ Remaining bent on a circle, staying straight on a straight line, and bending to other side.
■ Bending into leg-yielding.
■ Positioning into shoulder-in or travers from a straight line or on a circle and back.
■ Riding corners, circles, serpentines, and straight lines.

- Developing shoulder-in into half-pass, and back to a straight line.
- Correct canter into counter canter.

One can see that there is a definite progression in the difficulty of the demands in these transitions. And, this list can be extended as you move up from level to level.

Be very concerned with transitions, where they are and how to ride them, instead of simply memorizing the patterns. Good transtions lead to good movements—and good scores.

CHAPTER FOUR:

QUALITY OF GAIT

A N O T H E R key element in every test, as clearly shown by the definition in the AHSA *Rule Book* and on the test sheet itself, is the quality of gait in which movements and transitions must be shown. Since dressage riding is aimed at developing the natural gaits to their best, judges are looking closely for this quality.

There is a close relationship between the quality of the gaits and the ability to ride the movement and transitions required. What is basic to the quality of the gaits is the frame, self-carriage, and acceptance of the bit, which permit the movements and transitions to be correctly executed at any given level. You can ride a 20-meter circle on a light contact, but that light contact won't work for a 10-meter canter circle followed by a simple change. That movement requires, along with every movement and transition written into the test, a certain quality of gait. Without it, it is impossible to ride the movement or transition well.

Take, for example, a First Level movement, the lengthening of the stride in the trot. What counts is the transition in and out of the lengthening, and the quality of the trot in which the lengthening is shown. The actual length of the stride is not nearly as important as is the regularity of the rhythm, the lightness in front, and the steadiness on the bit. Unless there is a correct transition and quality of gait in the lengthening, the horse will never be able to progress to a correct medium gait in Second Level.

Quality of gait is a poorly understood concept, but once it is appreciated, it is easy to assess. It is not just a vague impression of the judge but, when understood, will help you evaluate your strong points and deficiencies. It will let you know when you are ready for a particular level.

There are eight elements to quality of gait:

- Rhythm
- Suppleness
- Straightness
- Acceptance of the bit
- Impulsion
- Collection
- Cadence
- Lightness

Remember, your ride is judged not only on the degree of exactness of the patterns and movements required, but also on these eight elements of the quality of gaits. Let's take a close look at each of these elements.

RHYTHM

It is primarily the regularity and correctness of the rhythm in every gait that is important. Once started, the same rhythm must be maintained throughout the movements: circles, turns, extensions, collection, working gaits, and so on. It is essential not to go any faster than the speed at which the horse can comfortably perform the movements.

It is a common mistake to increase the rhythm on a straight line and then reduce it for the next movement such as a corner, circle, shoulder-in, half-pass, etc. If we are asked to cover more ground or collect the horse, it is the length of stride that is adjusted, not the frequency of the steps. This applies equally to the walk, trot, and canter. Any deviation will reflect poorly in the score for the movement. Further, this also applies to shoulder-in, haunches-in, half-pass, turns on the haunches, and all the more advanced movements.

There are two basic deviations I see from correct rhythm. The first is a slowing down of the rhythm. This is most frequently seen in the down transitions from an extension to collection. Collection is not a slower pace; it is simply a shorter stride with more energy, engagement, and elevation. What is asked for is a change of stride and not of rhythm; we must always remember that.

This situation becomes worse when a reduction of stride is accompanied by a loss of regularity and purity of the gait. This is most frequently seen with pacing in the walk and a four-beat canter. When that happens, the collected marks for gaits may become as insufficient as the marks for the movement itself.

The second basic mistake I see is an increase in the rhythm, or running and rushing at its most extreme. This occurs frequently when lengthening or extension is called for with an incorrectly prepared horse. Once this rushing has started, it is nearly impossible to correct during the movement since the horse is almost always on the forehand. Especially when teaching lengthening of the stride or extensions, the regularity of rhythm is the single most important factor, and not the degree of lengthening achieved (which will gradually improve anyway). What is required is a lengthening of the stride generated by the engagement and thrust of the haunches and not the increase of speed and rhythm.

The last and probably least severe mistake I see is a temporary loss of regularity, or breaking of the rhythm, that may occur when asking too much of a young horse or when the ground and footing are not even. This is a situation where asking for a little less than maximum often brings better results than trying to go all out.

SUPPLENESS

Suppleness is a progressive achievement of correct training, the degree of which determines to a large extent the level at which a horse can be successfully shown.

Suppleness must be demonstrated laterally by the horse's ability to bend based on the degree of freedom in the shoulders. This, in turn, determines the degree to which two track and lateral movements are possible, as well as the size of circles and turns. The ability to bend must be developed equally to both sides even though every horse has a better side to begin with. Corners, serpentines, circles, shoulder-in, and half-pass are testing figures and are always symmetrical in a test. They will quickly expose any shortcomings of one side when compared with the other.

Suppleness also shows itself longitudinally; that is, the degree to which a horse can change his frame by lengthening and shortening. In addition, this suppleness is demonstrated by the ability not only to engage the haunches, but also by the angles of articulation in the hind legs to a degree that lowers the croup. This gives the impression of elevating the horse in front, and giving the rider the feeling that the horse is consistently in front of the rider's legs. The horse becomes truly collected and light on the bit. Some teachers refer to this longitudinal suppleness as the "accordion response" to proper aids.

The absence of longitudinal suppleness is particularly evident in the transitions from a long frame back to a more collected frame, or in the down. transitions from one gait to another. Here, a poorly-trained horse leans on the bit and goes on the forehand with a loss of

Longitudinal Suppleness

balance and rhythm. With the well-trained horse, the transition comes from behind.

Since in any dressage test there are three or four times more transitions than there are actual movements, it becomes immediately evident just how important it is to develop longitudinal as well as lateral suppleness of the horse in order to be able to ride a successful test.

STRAIGHTNESS

Absolute straightness is seen very rarely and usually only in very well-trained FEI level horses. It is, as everything else, a matter of degree. While hardly ever seen in young and green horses, straightness should become more and more evident as the training of the horse progresses. Straightness is the result of correct training with bending exercises and must be the goal for all three gaits.

Straightness is the ability of the horse to move well on a straight line as well as on a circle, with the inside hind leg following the front leg exactly on one track. Only this guarantees that the hind legs are correctly under the horse, and that the total thrust and power is not being dissipated laterally, but instead supports and drives the horse forward into the hands of the rider. Since there are so many straight sections to ride in the lower level tests, including the long sides, the diagonals and the centerline, the need to learn to ride straight can not be overemphasized. We will look at each of these straight sections individually in the chapter on movements.

ACCEPTANCE OF THE BIT

Unlike popular perception, acceptance of the bit has very little to do with the frame in which we ride the horse. It is more that wherever we place our reins–long, short, or to one side–the horse follows them without evasion. Acceptance of the bit could also be called "the confidence of the horse in the rider's hand."

Riding a horse in a very short and cramped frame in front has nothing to with being on the bit. Neither does work with draw reins, martingales, curbs, chambons and other artificial aids (based on inflicting pain) help to achieve it. The acceptance of the bit is a demonstration that the horse has been taught to find his balance and to carry himself willingly, accepting the reins and the bit as communication, rather than a threat of pain or support to lean on.

Only when the horse has accepted the bit can he begin to carry himself. And, as the engagement improves, the horse will become lighter and lighter, without the rider having to use any artificial aids or excessive rein action.

Without good hands, it is impossible to ride a horse on the bit, so don't blame your horse. If you run into difficulties, first look at what you are doing with your hands.

"Acceptance of the bit" as a requirement in the tests begins at Training Level and progresses until the horse is expected to be "on the bit" by Second Level.

The usual evasion to acceptance of the bit will be one of the following: The horse takes the bit, pulls the reins out of the rid-

er's hands, and thrusts his head up. This is frequently seen in transitions, and with riders who lack tact or feel in their hands. Or, the horse goes behind the bit, evading the hands of the rider and the influence of the reins. As with the first evasion, this behavior is an indication of poor training and poor hands. Both evasions are severely penalized in the movement itself, and if constant throughout the test, in the collective marks for the horse and rider.

A different situation is a horse that is behind the vertical, but basically accepting the bit. This is usually not an evasion on the part of the horse, but reflects poor horsemanship since it is the rider who holds the horse behind the vertical. This will also show up in the collective marks as well as in the score for the movements.

IMPULSION

Only once we have a steady rhythm, some suppleness and straightness, with the horse confirmed on the bit, can we begin to see real impulsion. Impulsion is the power from the haunches, driving and supporting the horse at the same time. While only minimal in the beginning, it will be seen more and more as training progresses and the difficulty of the test increases. Without impulsion, the higher tests simply cannot be ridden correctly and elegantly, and the expected quality of gait is missing.

COLLECTION

Collection is a combination of engagement and flexion of the haunches. Collection is nothing absolute but a matter of degree, conditioned by the ability of the horse and the requirements of the movement being executed. Collection goes hand in hand with impulsion. It starts with the first engagement as seen in turns and shoulder-in in the lower levels and culminates in the levade, where all the weight of the horse and rider is balanced on the flexed haunches directly under the center of

gravity. Collection ultimately becomes an automatic self-carriage of the horse when ridden with the proper aids and support.

Collection, first asked for at Second Level, is a progressive flexion and stepping under of the haunches on a circle or corner, but which can later be maintained on a straight line. True collection—elevation in front, lightness, and the horse truly in front of the rider's legs—is the last stage of development and the basis for all advanced movements.

Remember, collection has nothing to do with pulling in the horse's head and shortening the frame in front, nor can it be achieved by doing sitting trot on a straight line for hours.

CADENCE

Once we have the combination of rhythm, impulsion, acceptance of the bit, self-carriage and the ability to collect and extend, we can begin to see cadence, the true beauty of dressage riding, as far as gaits are concerned. Cadence is particularly evident in collected trot and passage, while it does not appear in piaffe, where there is no moment of suspension. Cadence and the suspension during the strides is

one of the goals for a young horse and an aspiring dressage competitor, but it is definitely outside of the frame of this guide for beginning competitors and work at lower levels.

LIGHTNESS

Even de la Gueriniere, the most sophisticated of the classical masters of equitation, lamented that there were hardly any truly light horses made anymore. So what is a truly light horse? Definitions in French, German and English literature vary greatly in their descriptions.

Generally speaking, lightness is a unity with the rider. The horse remains on a light contact on the bit, able to do whatever is asked of him, almost anticipating the movements, and allowing the rider to enjoy every stride of his performance, without any physical effort. However, it is only seen in those exceptionally athletic horses totally confirmed in all gaits, in self-carriage, and at ease with all movements asked. Once experienced, it is an unforgettable remembrance. Lightness is the ultimate in self-carriage, collection, acceptance of the aids and athletic ability.

Why don't we see true lightness more often? Because it is much easier to put the horse into a collected frame with "muscle," curb rein, and spurs, and ride Grand Prix, than to train a truly elegant horse for a light performance. It is the limitations of the rider that prevents the horse from performing at his best, namely light. But, this is way beyond the problems of beginners and will only become an objective once all the basic training elements have been mastered and the horse has become a true athlete, as well as having a natural talent for this type of work.

So, we see it is not only the execution of the movements and transitions, but the elements of the quality of gait that are evaluated by the judge to arrive at a fair assessment of the performance presented in front of him.

The further you advance, the more important the quality of gait becomes in comparison to execution and precision. Once you reach FEI level, it is not a question of just doing a correct flying change. What makes the difference between a five and an eight in the score is the quality of it.

THE WORKING GAITS

Working gaits are difficult to explain because we are not dealing with well-defined gaits like medium, collected, or extended gaits. Instead, we are dealing with a progressively improving acceptance of the bit and aids, reflected in the change in the horse's frame from Training Level to Second Level. This change must be in accordance with definitions of the AHSA levels, as previously discussed.

It is in the working gaits that the natural conformation of the horse, from Anglo-Arabs to Thoroughbreds to European Warm-bloods, present us with a bewildering variety of sights.

The schooling of dressage horses at this level is not unlike the training of young enlisted men who report to boot camp. Some men come in blue jeans, some in suits and ties. Some men have beards, some have long hair. Some wear sneakers, others wear cowboy boots. Some men are fat, some men are thin. Some are tall and some are small. But regardless of their differences, they all get a crew-cut, a uniform, and learn to obey their drill sergeat's instruction.

Gradually, they approach the desired standards, uniformity, and requirements which will turn them into useful soldiers. And so it is with horses.

The progression of this transformation is reflected in the standards of the levels, and the progressively more difficult tests. Circles get smaller and smaller, and the horse must go straighter and straighter. Changes must be made at the letter, not before or after. The walk is eliminated from the transition in and out of the halt. Obedience is required in bending, in rein backs, and in the turns on the haunches, with no resistance being shown. These movements will test the horse' s ability to respond to the rider's aids.

So what is the working gait, broadly defined? It is the progres-

Elevation

Collection

Suspension

Light in front

Impulsion

Sure
Footed

sive balance, self-carriage, obedience to the aids, straightness, acceptance of the bit, and the athletic ability of the horse to execute the more and more demanding movements and transitions without any apparent difficulty as he progresses from Training to Second Level.

These demands can be met at Training Level where 20-meter circles, sliding canter departs, and walk transitions in and out of the halt with the horse on a light contact are asked for. This becomes unacceptable, though, once we are required to ride straight lines, 10-meter circles, leg-yielding, and trot–canter–trot transitions, and so on.

This progression is usually easier for the European Warmblood because of his build than for the Arabian or Thoroughbred, who frequently considers being on the bit and aids a personal insult and behaves accordingly in the beginning. As long as we understand that working gaits are nothing absolute, but are instead a gradually changing configuration and frame of the horse as a result of his training, we have at least grasped the essentials. You should let the AHSA definitions of the various tests be your guide and the ease by which your horse can do the test be the measure of your progress.

If you read the AHSA *Rule Book*, you may be totally confused, as everyone else is, as to what a horse "on the bit" in relation to the working gaits actually means. Just forget it (it is quite likely that this definition will be changed anyway in the near future). To give you a little background: the definitions for working gaits were taken straight from the FEI *Rule Book* and, unfortunately, poorly translated. Furthermore, working gaits, as far as the FEI is concerned, only exist in the FEI Three Day Event Dressage test, and are roughly equivalent to Third or Fourth Level tests. For valid reasons, the FEI substituted the working gaits in those tests instead of collected gaits, in order to accommodate and do justice to the levels and requirements demanded in the training of event horses. There are no tests in Europe equivalent to our Training and First Level.

Furthermore, these definitions were never intended to be used

for American Training and First Level tests. This becomes obvious in the total absence in the AHSA Rule Book of any definition
for lengthening of the stride in the working trot or canter (a key
feature in the American tests), or any reference to the rising trot
except in a one-half line statement.

The best definition in the Rule Book refers to the working
walk, with the admonition to leave a good natural walk alone;
this cannot be taken seriously enough in this stage of training.

A WORD ABOUT RISING TROT

Although there is almost nothing mentioned about the rising trot
in the dressage section of the AHSA Rule Book, since much of the
trot work in Training Level and the lengthening of the trot in
First Level are done in rising trot, let's consider it for a moment.

Most instructors teach rising on the outside diagonal, when
the inside hind leg and the outside front leg are swinging forward
and are off the ground. This is a fine basic standard, easy to
remember and execute, and applicable if you are on the right or
left hand.

The classic definition from Museler says one sits either on the
inside hind leg or outside hind leg when trotting. However, since
most riders hardly know what's going on in front of them, much
less behind, I will refer to posting on the inside or posting on the
outside to differentiate between the two possibilities.

Nowhere in the English literature will you find a clear
rationale why you should post on the outside when learning to
ride or when training a young horse. The reason is very simple
and goes back to the days of the cavalry. Most horses, as we
know, are slightly crooked and will automatically sit a rider on
the diagonal they prefer. If this is done consistently on a green
horse, it will lead to the strengthening of the muscle on only one
side, ultimately accentuating the crookedness of the horse.
Having the rider post on the right as well as on the left side, and
not just on the side the horse prefers, assures equal muscular
development and may even contribute with other exercises to

developing straightness and self-carriage in the young horse. As a matter of fact, when training a horse, it does not matter which side you pick, the inside or outside diagonal, as long as you alternate it regularly. However, when riding in a test, additional considerations must enter our approach as we will see later.

Since there is no word in the *Rule Book* regarding which side is correct, nor any suggestions on the actual test sheets, you are theoretically free to post on either side. I would not recommend this, however, because in competition some judges still feel that only the outside is correct. But there is no basis for such a decision. To my mind, this is not an arbitrary omission; in the canter, for stance, there are very clear statements on which lead to ride: right, left, or counter-canter.

The type of posting traditionally taught is probably best for beginners, but the absence of a fixed rule does have advantages for the more sophisticated rider. In any young horse, we are concerned with the inside hind leg which we try to keep under the horse. If possible, we want this leg engaged, since it has to carry more weight in turns and circles, and can also help to position the horse on a straight line. Similarly, we want to support the inside shoulder in turns and circles, when all of the weight is on the inside front leg. Since the trot is a diagonal, two-beat gait, the inside hind leg swings forward when the inside front leg carries the weight. It is clear that on a young horse our aids can only affect the leg which carries no weight, and which is free to move forward and under the horse. There is nothing we can do at the moment those legs are carrying the total weight of the horse and rider.

Our aids to support the inside shoulder and to encourage more engagement and stepping under of the inside hind leg are a driving seat and increased leg pressure on the inside. Unfortunately, we are out of the saddle with our legs swinging away from the horse, exactly when we should use these aids, if we post on the "correct" outside diagonal. Contrarily, if we post on the inside diagonal, we are sitting in the saddle with our legs on the horse, able to apply our aids when the horse's weight is on the inside front leg, and the inside hind leg is swinging forward. Doing this deliberately will improve the horse's straighthess and gait, as well as the balance and support in bending in circles and turns.

You must decide for yourself whether or not to tempt the judges with posting on the "wrong" diagonal, since some of them may still want to penalize with a lower score due to an "error in execution." As for myself, I have always posted on the inside diagonal deliberately, since I am never too concerned with the score. I am more concerned with trying to support the horse when I feel he needs it most.

It does not matter on which side you post on crossing the arena on the diagonal and never change at X since it can disturb the balance and rhythm. But be sure to be more supportive in the turn onto the centerline where your horse needs all the help he can get.

This basic principle can be taken a step further to the warm up area if you do not wish to tire out your horse by too much sitting trot after having already shown him in one or two tests. If you want to practice leg-yielding on a circle, or shoulder-in on a circle or straight line, you can do it just as well rising on the inside

as in sitting trot, since you will be in the saddle when the aids must be there. Similarly, when you ride travers, you can post on the outside and the aids will be there when needed.

Therefore, if the horse needs support for the inside hind leg, you sit on the inside. If the haunches are failing out and you want to support the outside hind leg in a turn, you sit on the outside. It is as simple as that.

CHAPTER FIVE:

THE MOVEMENTS AND HOW TO RIDE THEM

THE basic movements in Training and First Levels are: walk on a straight line and through the corner; canter on both leads, including corners and circles; trot, including corners and circles to both sides; and halt. First Level adds leg-yielding to both sides, a movement that has been in and out of dressage tests for the last thirty years and is still rather controversial. First Level also adds lengthening of the strides in trot and canter. In Second Level we see added: travers, shoulder-in, and the counter-canter.

Looking at the movements by themselves, not much is asked of horse and rider as long as each movement is ridden by itself. A very green or young horse can execute the Training and First Level movements within a few months after starting his initial training.

Why then do we see so many poor tests even at these lower levels? All that is required upon entrance into the ring is a halt, walk, trot, canter, then an exit. Obviously, the difficulty is not in the movements themselves but in the way the movements are arranged within the test, which require the rider to perform and ask his horse for transitions. If the rider only practices the individual movements at home rather than in sequence as in the test, the competition will quite likely be a disaster.

It the rider understands this situation, and practices the transitions as carefully as the particular movement, he will quickly understand that there can be a world of difference in the way one movement flows into the next and in the degree of proficiency that is required to do well in a test.

With that in mind, let's look at many of the movements individually.

The Entry on the Centerline

When looking at the ring before the test, take a very good look at the centerline and the area around A. Every test reads the same:

A   Enter...
X   Halt, Salute, Proceed...
C   Turn...

This is certainly one of the most difficult movements at any level and will be your personal calling card on the judge–a dead give-away of your and your horse's ability. So you must ride it well. It should be practiced at home again and again since from Training Level up to Grand Prix you will ride a minimum of two but often more centerlines per test.

But, first, you must correctly get on the centerline and this is where most amateurs fail. Only a good look at the entrance to the ring and A will give you the answer. So start with the following basic concepts:

1. The entrance to the ring is not geometrically in the center of the short side.

2. A is not the center of the opening.

3. The judge sits at C and has an absolutely perfect view of the line from A to C which is not necessarily in the true sense the geometric centerline of the ring.

4. The test reads "Enter at A," not in the middle of the opening of the ring or the geometrically exact centerline.

5. If the first rider makes a mistake and enters off the centerline, usually everyone else in the class follows the same incorrect track. Therefore, when you approach the centerline at A, always assume that the riders ahead of you were wrong and ride your own line. Also, remember that after ring maintenance, the letter A may no longer be in the same spot as before when you looked at the arena.

So where is the line A to C in relation to the opening in the ring? In 80 percent of the rings I've seen, either to the left or to the right of the center and that is where you have to come in and not in the middle of the gate. Make yourself a mental note of the spot in the gate that is exactly on the line A to C.

Looking at the figure, note that if you enter through the middle of the gate, you are already off the centerline before you even start your test. Whatever you do later, you are definitely down one point on your first move.

There are two correct ways to enter:

The first is on the better bend or lead of the horse, either from the right or the left, but always inside of A.

If there is no room, or uneven footing or mud puddles, or the letter A is too close to the ring, walk straight up to A, line up on the line from A to C, and just go straight for X and C and the judge when you are ready. If you want, you can halt at A outside the ring, or simply enter in the trot from the walk. This entry was used even at the Olympics in Los Angeles and the last World Championships.

Never try to maneuver outside of the letter A with a young horse, swinging back in, bending the other way and then straightening out. You won't be able to do it unless you have an advanced FEI horse and it doesn't look pretty either.

Frankly, there are so many ways to start your test badly that I

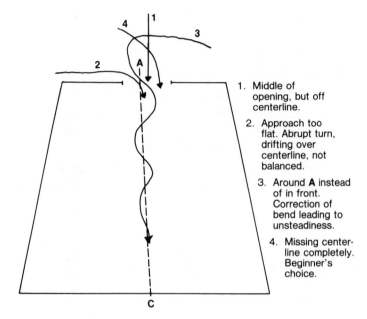

1. Middle of opening, but off centerline.

2. Approach too flat. Abrupt turn, drifting over centerline, not balanced.

3. Around **A** instead of in front. Correction of bend leading to unsteadiness.

4. Missing centerline completely. Beginner's choice.

Incorrect way to enter ring.

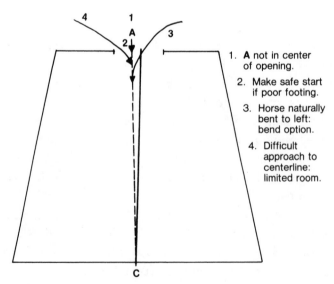

1. **A** not in center of opening.

2. Make safe start if poor footing.

3. Horse naturally bent to left: bend option.

4. Difficult approach to centerline: limited room.

Correct way to enter ring.

can't enumerate them all here. So concentrate only on how to do it right, and decide how you will do it when you look at the ring on your first inspection.

As you come down the centerline, the judge should only see the front legs and between them the tail; the hind legs should be moving exactly behind the front legs, practically invisible. It is from this straightness that the halt has to be developed and, in order not to disturb the balance, the halt should be made with your seat against holding hands and not by pulling back.

If there is only one judge (at C), it is impossible to see if the halt is really at X. So it's more important to concentrate on the straight, smooth transition from behind to a straight halt. Also, with an absolutely straight view from the font, the judge cannot tell if the forelegs are absolutely square. And, since the hind legs are not visible, no judge can see if they are really square or not either.

Above all, once you have made the halt, don't try to make any corrections; it almost always makes matters worse.

When you have two judges, your halts must be square and straight from the side as well as from the front. A common fault is to come to a halt two or three meters before or after X. There is really no excuse for this and the score may reflect different views from the judge at E or B and the judge at C. One may give you a 3 or 4 and other an 8, due to the difference in the angle of vision.

How To Halt At X

When viewed from the side, or judged from E or B, 90 percent of all halts ridden are between one and five meters before or after X. In addition, the riders usually realize too late that they are over the mark. Then, this realization results in an abrupt transition, finishing with a horse that is neither square in front or in back, and a horse that leans heavily on the forehand.

When you reach qualifying and finals classes, you must satisfy the judge at E or B, as well as the one at C. It doesn't matter how good your halt may look from C; the judge at B will rate your halt either a 3 or 4 if not performed satisfactorily.

There is a very simple way to avoid this dilemma at X and to end up exactly on it, without even looking. Ride your horse from A to X, forward and on the bit, and in the gait required by the test. Have a ground person (or yourself) count the number of strides from the point the horse enters the ring to the exact point where the front legs strike X. Good movers usually have 20 or 21 trot strides, average horses 24 to 27, and small horses and ponies anything from 27 strides on up. Repeat the entrance several times, until the rhythm, scope and number of strides is always the same. You will then be at X every time exactly at the same stride. If you are required to enter in the canter, remember that the canter strides are much longer, and for an average horse, about 12 canter strides will be needed.

Assuming you reach X consistently at the 23rd stride, you can enter as follows: Count the strides from the point of entry up to 18. At the 19th stride, give the first half halt; at the 22nd stride give the second half halt, and at the 23rd, ride the full halt, from behind into your hands, followed by a short release without letting the horse fall apart). You will be exactly at X and on a square horse, which is ready to move on at your command, without having to look around to make sure you are on X.

This approach takes the guess work out of the centerline, giving you confidence and your horse balance. The result will be two good scores from the judges at E and C.

SQUARE HALTS

Asking for a square, straight halt only at the show never works. It takes practice and a good teacher from the ground to help with the proper corrections of your seat and the center of gravity for you and your horse.

The difficulty with the halt is that most of them are not straight and, when not straight, they are obviously not going to be square. If the legs are not properly lined up, the slightest deviation from a proper halt becomes instantly visible to the judge at C.

In most cases when this happens, the horse's haunches swing to the left, and/or the left hind leg steps out. There is an explanation for this that may give a clue to how to correct it. Most horses are bent naturally to the left and sit their riders to the left of the center of gravity for their own comfort. At the halt, the horse's center of gravity is shifted slightly to the left. As the horse tries to step under the center of gravity, he moves his haunches left for support. In addition, most riders are right-handed and use more pressure on the right rein. By this unintentional indirect rein action, the rider blocks the last half step of the left hind leg which, instead of moving under the horse, moves laterally to support the weight and stays behind. One way to correct this is to sit deliberately to the right and, when coming to a halt, release the right rein slightly more than the left. If the problem is crookedness on the other side, reverse the aids.

If this does not help, have an experienced ground person or trainer observe you and your horse and suggest ways to help you correct this basic fault. It's too important to leave it up to luck!

Also remember that when a horse moves off from a halt, by moving one front leg, he must rebalance himself on the three other legs. He does this by shifting his weight back and laterally, using his head and neck. If the rider does not allow this, perhaps in the mistaken impression that the horse must be "held" on the bit, the transition will be a falling motion with short steps to the right or left but not straight forward.

Riding From X to C

When coming to a halt, you should put your horse together from behind as much as possible by riding your halt with your seat. This way, you have the horse in front of your legs and straight, and the transition to the trot from the halt will be instantaneous, straight, and coming from behind without any walk steps in between. If you ride your horse "with your hands," your horse will most likely fall on the forehand, the haunches escaping, and avoiding engagement by staying behind or falling to the left or right. And this is a terrible position to be in for a clean transition to the trot. A crooked horse on the forehand needs a few walk steps to get back into the trot. The combination of a crooked and not-square halt and an up transition through the walk doesn't rate much more than a 4 even at First Level.

Once the halt has been made, be it good, bad or so-so, don't try to correct it. Everybody has already seen it; and moving after the halt has been established will just cost you another point. You must make the best of an otherwise bad situation.

Smile, relax, take all the time in the world, and salute. Nobody in the world can push you. Not your mother, not the judge, not the steward, not your teacher, not the show management. From hereon, you are the boss and you decide what you are going to do, and when, and how. From the time you make your halt until you move on, you should be able to count to 20 without rushing. There is plenty to be done anyway.

First, wait until your horse gets light on the bit in your steady hands before you move your right hand to salute. Too often I see horses tossing their heads as soon as the right hand is taken off and there goes a decent transition into the trot!

Second, when putting the rein back into the right hand, get organized. Be sure your horse is still on the bit, the reins are of equal length, and you are sitting straight and comfortable. Take all the time in the world.

Third, you must know while you are at X at what speed and rhythm you will take off in order to make a good turn at C. You must be sure that you are not going faster than you can handle all the movements before the first lengthening or canter transition is required. This decision at X will determine to a very large degree the first three or four scores you receive.

When riding to C, indicate to your horse with a little vibrating reins that the time has come to move. Then use your seat and legs, just giving a fraction of an inch with your fingers to allow the horse to rebalance himself and to get an instantaneous and powerful transition, straight forward from behind, and in a good trot.

The problems I see with young horses between X and C are many, but the most frequent are a progressive reluctance to move forward, a tendency to slow down, and evasions. There is a progressively increasing desperation of the rider as the pair comes closer to C and the judge. But look at it from the horse's point of view: Why should he be ridden full speed ahead into a contraption in which he has been brought to the show, a trailer, and one which in addition is already fully occupied? Your horse is definitely smarter than you are in his own way, so what is the solution?

You must tell your horse as early as a few steps after X that you will turn right or left. Shift to the new inside and keep your horse straight with your outside rein and inside leg. Vibrate your inside rein a bit so your horse knows what you expect a moment later, and nurse your young horse down the centerline step by step until you give in and begin turning. Sometimes you may have to give in and turn earlier than you might want, but this is far better than to run into resistance, loss of rhythm, and a rattled horse and rider before you even begin your test.

A common mistake before the turn at C is to drift off the centerline in the opposite direction. This becomes very visible particularly when turning to the right on a horse that turns better to the left. One often sees riders sitting to the outside of the turn and the horse drifting to the left and out of control. If this happens, the horse gains one or two meters for his turn, which must be penalized. Further, the horse is usually off balance, insufficiently bent, falling on the right shoulder, and therefore unable to perform the first turn

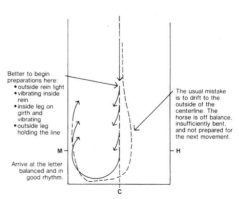

Better to begin
preparations here:
 • outside rein light
 • vibrating inside
   rein
 • inside leg on
   girth and
   vibrating
 • outside leg
   holding the line

Arrive at the letter
balanced and in
good rhythm.

The usual mistake
is to drift to the
outside of the
centerline. The
horse is off balance,
insufficiently bent,
and not prepared for
the next movement.

M —

— H

C

on a single clean track or within the 10 meters allocated for this movement. The judge's score will be accordingly low.

If we look at the total problems inherent in riding the center-line, there is no wonder that there are more 4's than 10's in the scoring. But since this is one of the most repeated movements in tests, you must practice and learn to ride it correctly in order not to lose points show after show.

The Turn at C

Depending on how it is ridden, the turn at C can be either a disaster or the best thing that was ever put into a test. Unfortunately, few amateurs and beginners know how to use this movement to full advantage and so lose points, not only for the movement itself but for the one that follows.

Looking at this movement from its geometrical configuration, it is immediately clear that any beginner or young horse up to Second Level can only ride it as a 10-meter half-circle.

Riding one-quarter of a 6-meter turn at C, then riding straight, followed by another one-quarter of a 6-meter circle in the corner is beyond the ability of even most advanced riders and horses. We must remember that the first time a 6-meter circle, or part of it, was required was at Intermediate II but it is not required in any FEI level test today. So why ask a lower level horse to do something he obviously cannot yet do, and that will only teach him to evade by falling on his shoulder, or losing the haunches, along with any semblance of balance, regularity, rhythm and confidence?

For a young or inexperienced rider, or for a young or inexperienced horse, the only sensible option is a 10-meter half-circle. It will be difficult enough to ride this half-circle properly—balanced, with correct bend, on one track, with no change in rhythm, and the inside hind legs supporting more weight without evasion—and to arrive at M or H, with the horse in a better frame and balance than when leaving at X.

Your chance to succeed depends on the speed and rhythm you

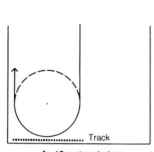

As 10-meter circle.

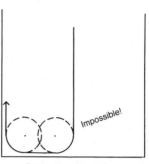

As two 6-meter circles.

choose for the take-off at X. This will not only determine the turn itself but will significantly influence the score of the next movement.

If you arrive at M (or H) on a balanced horse in a steady rhythm, the next movement will be smooth, supple and balanced, and you will get good marks. However, if you fail in your turn, coming out off-balance, it will take you four or more strides to get your horse back physically. But you may never regain his confidence after he has been ridden into an impossible situation on the first turn of the test for absolutely no good reason.

The practical way to go about it is really very simple:

- Know the speed and rhythm at which you can handle a 10-meter circle and the movements ahead and don't exceed it at the transition at X into the trot.

- Indicate to your horse if you will go to the right or left, and aim inside the letter C.

- The closer you get to G, develop a shoulder-fore position but keep your outside leg on the horse to avoid drifting off the centerline to the outside (a very common mistake of 50 to 60 percent of all riders).

This drifting out will cost you at least a point, since you are not only off the centerline, but reducing significantly the degree of difficulty in the turn at C by enlarging the 10-meter half-circle to 11 or 12-meters.

To continue,

■ Start your half-circles at G, which is 6 meters from C. Since the track is roughly two feet inside the enclosure, you will be just about right. Look at M and shift your weight to the inside; your horse will do the rest by himself if kept in the same bend as in the shoulder-fore.

Usually, however, after a long straight centerline with lots of transitions, the horse will be strung out by the time he reaches G. So this half-circle is also your chance to put the horse back in a tighter frame.

Further, if you start your half-circle properly at G after preparing for it on the centerline—keeping your outside leg back and using your inside leg against your outside rein after a half halt at G—you will find your horse in a much better frame and balance at M or H than when you rode off at X.

From then on, the rest of the test should be fun; it's not an exaggeration that the quality of the centerline and first turn determine in large part the results of the first half of your test, and the basic impression you make on the judge.

The Long Side: Riding Straight

In most lower level tests, after the turn at C you have a straight section from M or H to B or E, or even F or K. This movement is away from the judge's view and the position and straightness of the horse is very visible from behind.

Riding with the outside of the horse parallel to the enclosure of the ring guarantees that your horse will be crooked, with his haunches falling in and the inside hind legs stepping laterally forward and not under the horse. This is so obvious that it is

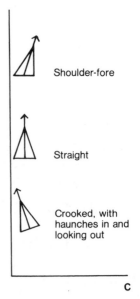

Shoulder-fore

Straight

Crooked, with haunches in and looking out

C

impossible to overlook from C and applies to all three gaits.

The reason for this rather disappointing fact is that the front and shoulders of the horse are much narrower than the rump. We can best compare it to a pyramid when seen from above as in the illustration.

Since straightness is one of the basic requirements of dressage riding, showing a crooked horse this way does not add to your scores at all. In addition, it makes any transition to a turn, a circle, or any other movements so much more difficult that the chance to do it well decreases very rapidly. The section from H or M to E and B away from the judge must not only be ridden correctly, but you must at the same time prepare your horse for the transition at E or B.

A practical and simple way to accomplish this by an inexperienced rider or young horse is as follows:

■ As you come out of the turn at C, don't let the horse just go down the track. Keep the bend a little, staying in a shoulder-fore position.

■ Maintain the shoulder-fore position for the entire distance so that your horse's outside haunches are closer to the ring than his outside shoulders. This way, you ensure that the point of the pyramid is exactly over the center of the base, and moving straight, with the inside hind legs stepping under the body of the horse and not out laterally.

The fact that the horse looks slightly to the inside can easily be corrected later by using a little more outside rein.

Basically, the degree of straightness required can be defined as follows: in a Training Level horse, we do not expect to see real straightness, though a relatively straight horse certainly gets a bonus point, as well as the rider who makes an honest effort to get it. By Training Level 3 or 4, we expect a little more straightness than in Training Level 1 or 2.

By First Level, we may not yet be able to take the shoulder-fore bend out of the horse, but the rider should at least place his horse's shoulders in front of his rear end and be able to move on one track, even if still slightly crooked. This is true for trot, but even more so for the canter.

By Second Level, there is no excuse for not riding absolutely straight to both sides, without bending, without the shoulder-fore positioning. We should see a straight horse who is steady on the bit and on the outside rein. If you can't do this, you are not yet ready for this level

In the higher levels, the concept of straightness is even more demanding as defined in the handbook of the German National Equestrian Federation, *Advanced Techniques of Riding*, in the section on dressage. It reads, "The straight line of the spine, as such, is not sufficient and cannot fulfill the requirement put upon straightness in dressage. That means that on all straight and curved lines the inside hind leg follows in the exact track of the inside front leg. The horse's outside hind leg is encouraged to move into the direction between the two front legs." This results in a "stepping under" the center of gravity and the horse moving more narrow behind. Any horse moving wide behind, or moving wider when asked to perform a lengthening, medium, or extended gait, is marked down for both movement and gaits. Here again, it does not get easier as we move up the scale in competitive dressage.

When approaching the turn or circle at B or E, increase the degree of the shoulder-fore position for one stride. Sit to the inside and use your inside leg against the outside rein as much as possible. You will find the difficulty of the subsequent movement enormously reduced. A 10-meter circle suddenly feels like you have meters to spare, and the turn, even when done into empty space, does not give you the feeling of helplessly drifting over the outside shoulder.

Remember, you must set your horse up for the next movement when turning at C, riding absolutely straight in a shoulder-fore position. In this way, you will have a straight and balanced horse, ready for the transition into a circle or turn.

And if your take-off from X was correct in speed and rhythm, you will still be trotting in exactly the same way, going like a clock, which is really a happy feeling indeed!

Lengthening of the Trot on the Diagonal

Since lengthening of the stride is required in trot and canter in lower level tests, we must understand the basic difference between developing a lengthening from a working gait, and that of a medium or extended gait from collection as required in Second and Third Levels.

The latter is actually much simpler because we are starting with a horse that is already collected under himself, light, and in front of the rider' s leg. It is simply a matter of releasing the pushing energy of the haunches and combining it with the freedom of the shoulder to establish a true medium or extended gait.

On the other hand, the requirement of lengthening in the lower levels is to test that a horse has reached the degree of balance and freedom of movement necessary to demonstrate longer or shorter strides while still maintaining the rhythm, regularity, straightness and acceptance of the bit. This is not so difficult in the canter. In the trot, though, the situation is different. The difficulty is that the lengthening must be ridden from a working trot which is a free, forward-moving gait where the horse moves well in his own balance.

Frequently, asking for too much too quickly results in rushing and a loss of balance with faster, and often shorter, strides instead of the opposite. Lengthening of the trot can be more easily shown from a shortened trot by simply allowing the horse to go back to his natural stride, but this is actually a "false" lengthening. Moving from a natural working stride into a true lengthening is ideal, but more difficult to accomplish. In an actual competitive situation, it is often wise to use a combination of both approaches.

The key to success is, as always, proper preparation. The correct preparation for lengthening in a test situation actually starts on the opposite long side using whatever movement is requested, such as a circle, shoulder-in, or simply a shoulder-fore position, to enhance the engagement of the inside hind quarters.

The corner should be used to increase the engagement by

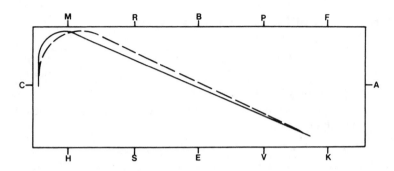

using your inside leg against your outside rein, and to shorten the gait a little bit by slight half halts, balancing the horse as much as possible coming out of the corner. On the short side it is essential to maintain this engagement with a slight shoulder-in or shoulder-fore position until you repeat the same exercise in the next corner to obtain the maximum energy and engagement possible in the young or green horse.

After the corner, the first important thing is to put the horse straight on the diagonal. Only at this point, when he is really balanced, should you apply the driving aids against soft hands, with gradually releasing fingers in order to let the energy go forward while maintaining control over rhythm, regularity and straightness.

With some horses (and experienced riders), you will see the lengthening, medium, or extended trot fully developed and asked for in the corner from a perfectly engaged and strong inside hind leg. This allows them to show a correct gait exactly at the letter instead of a few strides later. However, this is more difficult to ride and is, for the most part, beyond the capability of a young or inexperienced horse who is not yet muscled up behind. These horses need all the balance they can muster to ride a correct corner.

Never "drop" your horse at this time by giving the reins away. It is at this moment that he needs all the support you can give him so as not to leave the haunches behind and lose the entire preparation you put into the movement on the short side. Note that if you depend on a reader to know what to do and where to go, it will most likely be too late for these preparations.

If you get a good lengthening, go all the way to H. The closer you get to the judge, the more you are able to show how good you are.

The real difficulty in the lengthening comes in the down transition. If your horse is relatively well engaged, staying in a nice correct rhythm and remaining in front of your legs, your transition at H can be well done.

If your transition is too late, it will be very difficult to catch the horse when he is already going into the corner turn. The horse will probably be off balance and will run through the short side of the arena.

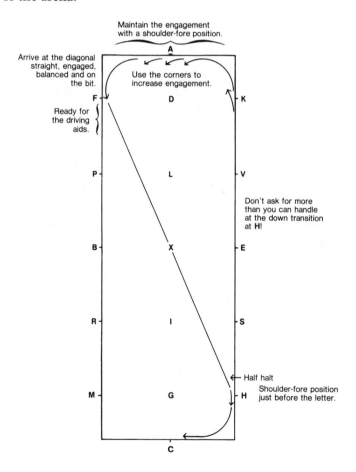

On the other hand, if your horse is rushing, off balance, on the forehand, and losing rhythm and regularity, it is far better to start your transition to the working trot way ahead of H. You will get an insufficient mark anyway, so you should concentrate on getting your horse back into a correct frame in the working trot so the movements that follow will not also be ruined by an out of control horse.

In principle, it is always wiser to use a movement that has already fallen apart to make the needed correction, and thereby preserve your chance at the next movement.

A sure sign that you're asking for too much too soon and your horse is insecure in his balance is that when asked to lengthen, he begins to move wide behind. Unfortunately, once a horse picks up this habit he will most likely keep it; it's very difficult to correct.

Another serious fault in lengthening, and seen even more frequently in the medium and extended trot, is "flicking" in front. What happens is that the front legs are extending but the hind legs cannot because the rider is holding the horse too tight and short in front. The front legs must return to the same shorter length of stride as the hind legs, since the front end of the horse cannot move away from his rear end by taking larger strides. It's a physical impossibility.

While this looks impressive to an uneducated observer, this is a sign of a basic shortcoming in training: a lack of true impulsion, engagement, and extension of the stride by the hind legs, and a restricted head and neck position which result in the front legs moving back from their original extension. There is an old saying that a horse cannot extend beyond his nose.

Once acquired, "flicking" is a difficult problem to correct. But it can be avoided in the early stages of training by allowing a longer frame when asking for the lengthening, medium or extended trot. Developing true impulsion and engagement will eliminate the problem altogether.

A special problem arises in arenas set up on an even slight hill or slant. Almost half of all horses will break or have a poor transition at the downhill end when asked for a maximum lengthening, medium or extended trot. But when moving in the uphill direction, they will do better than usual. So be circumspect and cautious when lengthening downhill, and almost reckless when going the other direction.

The Shoulder-in

The shoulder-in asked for in Second Level Tests 1, 2 and 3 are set up in the easiest way possible: coming out of the corner or after a circle.

The correct way to demonstrate and present a shoulder-in is stated eloquently in recent publications, in the *Rule Book*, and in any number of books on dressage riding. But the key to riding the shoulder-in correctly is to prepare it in the turn or circle so that your horse will have an engaged inside hind leg. You then ride the horse with your seat forward, between your inside leg and outside rein. Your inside rein, incidentally, is really only for decoration and for minor corrections.

The most common mistake is an improperly prepared horse being pulled by the inside rein in an awkward flexion of the neck, usually coming above the bit, and with the legs going relatively straight down the track.

Incidentally, if you follow the original description by de la Gueriniere and Steinbrecht on how to ride a shoulder-in, you will shift your weight slightly to the outside after establishing the shoulder-in position. De la Gueriniere, who was the first to describe how to properly execute a shoulder-in (in 1729), suggested sitting slightly to the outside by simply looking down the long side and not at your horse in order to maintain a straight track.

By doing so, you will help your horse "follow" you down the long side, with his center of gravity always slightly ahead of him and supported on the inside by your steady leg, with no chance to drift off the track or fall in. More often than not, the rider sits too much to the inside, actually pulling the horse with him off the track.

The aids as described by de la Gueriniere and Steinbrecht prevent the rider's inside leg from slipping back and therefore preventing the very common picture of the rider's toes turning out and the spurs going in. When this happens, the horses haunches drift out and the shoulder-in deteriorates into a leg-yield, which should result in a score of 4 at best. What I see, when this happens, is that the rider begins to use excessive hand aids which leads to a totally disorganized movement. A simple way for beginners and young horses to avoid this is for the rider to make a bridge between both reins, with the inside rein shorter. If the reins are held this way throughout the length of the movement, the bend of the horse will remain unchanged. With the outside rein held against the horse's neck, the correct position will be consistently held.

An altogether different problem is the transition out of the shoulder-in. The easiest way out is to move onto a circle, as in Second Level Test 4, where all you have to do is ease up on your inside leg and begin the circle.

A more difficult transition is when the shoulder-in finishes just before a corner. The easy way to approach this is to simply ride past the letter in a shoulder-in position and go around the corner as if you were going onto a circle. This, however, is not correct and avoids the difficulty put into the movement; a good judge will take notice.

If you read Second Level Tests 1 carefully, you will see that the movement ends at the letter R or S, just before the corner. This means that the front of your horse must be brought back to the track exactly in front of his hind legs before engaging into the turn, straight and on a single track.

Unless the transitions in and out of the shoulder-in are correct, scores of 7 or 8 are impossible, regardless of how good the shoulder-in itself might look.

While the correct definition of a shoulder-in is "a three track movement at about a 30 degree angle," it can only be assessed accurately by the judges at H or M. Because of the angle of vision at C, some additional considerations should be taken into account, as illustrated in the following example.

Judging at a judges' clinic with one of the outstanding I Level judges at C and with myself at H, we gave a shoulder-in from E to H a 5 and an 8 respectively. There was no question in my mind that the shoulder-in was good, almost very good. But my colleague at C said "inadequate angle and insufficient bend." Comparing the videos taken from behind both of us, the correctness of the movement was simply not visible from C. What are the conclusions? I suggest that you exaggerate your angle in competition to approximately 35 degrees.

When moving away from the judge at C, 35 degrees, or even up to 40, is a good idea. Otherwise, the rear end of your horse blocks the view of your movement, and at a 25 or 30 degree angle the judge will be disappointed.

On the other hand, when moving towards the judge you can be easier on the angle, with about 30 degrees in the far part of the ring, but moving to 35 degrees after E and B.

Above all, concentrate on steadiness, rhythm and lightness, and show an equal shoulder-in to both sides. It will cost you points if you show a good shoulder-in to one side and a poor one to the other. Your horse must be equally supple to both sides to be competitive.

The Travers (or Haunches-in)

Interestingly enough, in the time of classical riding the travers was considered a movement for improperly trained horses and poor riders. This was because in travers one could use the enclosure of the arena as an additional aid. Renvers, on the other hand, was considered to be correct and a true test (and proof!) of the ability of a horse and rider. Today, though, renvers is not required in National Tests.

But travers, if done correctly, demonstrates the horse's obedience and suppleness and the rider's adequate skill for the level of showing.

Once travers has been established, it is easier to keep the position and angle than it is in the shoulder-in since, in addition to our own aids, we have the enclosure of the arena to keep us on the track. So just concentrate on the angle, position, rhythm, acceptance of the bit, lightness, elegance and brilliance. This is certainly an easy movement to pick up a few points.

There is just no way to "slide" into a corner or a circle from the travers and look halfway good and come out on a balanced horse. In a travers, you have no choice: you must straighten out either shortly before or, at the latest, at the letter if you do not want to ruin your next turn or circle. Travers is first asked for from a 10-meter circle at V or P, and finishes at S or R, well ahead of the corner to rebalance the horse properly.

A further consideration is the angle of vision of the judge. In the AHSA *Rule Book*, a 30 degree angle is recommended for travers. This is fine when you are moving away from the judge. In addition, particularly in the upper part of the ring, the judge at C can only see your back and the rump of the horse, and has no possibility to assess what is going on in front. The important feature for the judge to assess, then, is the regularity and rhythm, and the position of the hind quarters, so concentrate on that.

Riding the travers towards the judge at C is totally different. The judge has a complete view of the transition into the travers and the transition out; he can see your seat, aids, legs, hands, the acceptance of the bit, rhythm, length of stride, impulsion and lightness–in short, everything. Therefore, don't dismiss the travers as an easy movement just because you got a 7 in another test where you rode away from the judge.

THE TRAVERS TRANSITION

In Second Level Test 4, the travers finishes at the letters M or H; in other words, six meters before the end of the arena. In no test does the travers finish in the corner. This is exactly what we must avoid, even though this makes a transition more difficult.

The test asks that your travers begin from a circle at E or B and finishes in the corner at H, or M. Since your travers starts at the letter where your circle finishes, you simply retain the bend when coming back on the track. Be certain, though, to give your horse a chance to gain his balance. Use a more demanding inside leg for one stride after the horse has been leaning in on the circle before using your outside leg; this will prevent the horse from falling over his inside shoulder. This transition has to be fast, accurate and balanced. Consciously or unconsciously, many riders make this transition easier for themselves and their horses by riding an oval instead of a circle. This obviously takes the difficulty out of a 10- or 8-meter circle and, in addition, gives them several strides to establish a new balance and the travers. But, this "oval" circle is just as insufficient by avoiding the difficulty of the test requirement as riding outside of X and the centerline would be. Furthermore, your transition into the travers is much easier than intended by the test. Depending how blatant the oval was and how visible from C, this may lead to a deduction of at least two points, or even "insufficient." If the oval is not too exaggerated, it is sometimes difficult to see from C, but you will be keenly disappointed in qualifying or finals classes when a knowledgeable judge at E or B gives you a 3 or 4 for the circle and a 5 for the travers with the comment that you avoided the difficulties of the test.

On the other hand, coming in a travers towards the corner, don't just ride past the letter and throw the horse around the corner, riding half of it on two tracks. Straighten your horse one stride before the letter and then ride a properly bent horse on one track through the corner to the short side.

When ending a shoulder-in or a travers, it is always the shoulders that are realigned to the haunches, and not the other way around. That means that in a shoulder-in, the front of the horse is brought back onto the track. When in travers, the front is moved off the track in front of the haunches.

The Circle

The circle is the most versatile geometric configuration in riding dressage and, as a judge, one can only marvel at the imagination of competitors on how to add a new twist to this apparently simple figure!

Every test contains circles: large ones, small ones, some placed in difficult spots, some very easy ones, and some placed before or after a transition into the next movement. But all of them have a number of basic requirements:

■ Circles must be round and executed exactly as stated in the test. This means the rider has to know where the "points" are. The rider must touch these points for one stride only.

■ They must be ridden on one track. This means that the horse must be able to bend and have sufficient freedom of the shoulders and hips to accommodate the requested size of the circle without the haunches falling out or the horse "popping" his shoulder.

■ The regularity of the rhythm must be the same throughout the circle, including engagement and impulsion, while the horse stays on the bit. As a matter of fact, the horse should be in a better frame coming out of the circle than going into it.

Circles present a golden opportunity in a test to put a horse together after a difficult preceding movement or to prepare the horse for the next one. This is something rarely used by inexperienced riders but consistently executed by professionals and experienced competitors.

THE 20-METER CIRCLE

The 20-meter circle of Training Level tests is executed at the end of the arena at A or at C, or at B or E. It is ridden exactly the same in both trot and canter. The following basic concepts will help to execute it properly. The horse should always be bent to the inside with the rider using the inside leg against the outside rein, and maintaining the same position throughout the entire circle.

There are four points that define the circle ridden at the ends of the arena. The center of the short side (A or C). The lateral points which are 4 meters above H and M or K and F. These are the most important points, and there is only one evenly bent line between them and the center of the short side. This line is inside the usual track on which we ride the corners. The next point is on the centerline, 2 meters beyond I or L. If you ride in an even bend through these four points, you can be certain the circle is absolutely round. It will also be much easier for the horse since he does not have to continuously change position or angle.

The most common mistake is to stick to the long side for four or five steps. The next most common is to ride a regular corner at H, F or K. When ridden like this, the circle resembles a squashed rectangle with irregularly rounded corners–certainly an insufficient performance.

To avoid the problem with the horse that sticks to the "wall" of the enclosure, I recommend that you ride your circle slightly inside the regular track. The horse is then deprived of the outside support and of sticking to it, and will continue in the same bend and rhythm without objection. And, by doing this

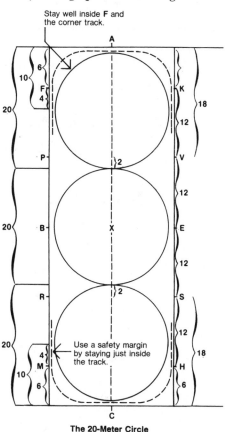

Stay well inside **F** and the corner track.

Use a safety margin by staying just inside the track.

The 20-Meter Circle

you will have a chance to improve your horse's frame and engagement during the entire movement. This is particularly important for young horses. Once a certain degree of training and higher levels of competition are reached, it is of lesser importance but still very often practiced by experienced riders. The advantage is that if you ride a nice, smooth, round circle, it will make it much easier for your horse to get engaged, collected, balanced and ready for the next movement. If you ride an uneven, rounded-square in between going straight, crooked or on a bend, and by changing the bend continuously, you will never be able to put the horse together for what is coming next.

SMALLER CIRCLES

Progressively smaller circles are more difficult to ride, not only because of the ability of the horse, but also in how they must be planned in advance. Again, the main thing is to know exactly where your points are. A 15-meter circle, for instance, does not go beyond a line halfway between X and E or B. A 10-meter circle never exceeds the centerline and an 8-meter circle is two meters inside of the centerline.

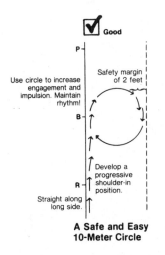

**A Safe and Easy
10-Meter Circle**

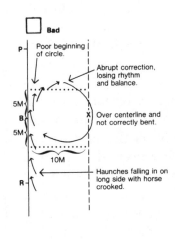

Exceeding these points reduces the difficulty of the movement, avoids the test requirements, and is insufficient irrespective of how well the circle is executed. And, since exceeding the points reduces the difficulty of the movement intended for the level of competition, it also demonstrates the inability of the rider to properly position his horse and should, in my opinion, also affect the collected marks of the rider.

It's a good idea when you ride a circle, particularly a 10- or 8-meter circle, to assume that the riders ahead of you were going too large and not really round. Always ride your own track and get a good result with a good score.

You can always stay inside the required maximum diameter by doing the following: Start your circle intentionally smaller than stated; for instance, 8 1/2 to 9 meters for a 10-meter circle. Horses tend to drift out and this technique gives you a one-meter safety margin if needed. If everything goes well, on the other hand, you can apply more driving aids to gain impulsion and engagement and let your horse go out on a slightly larger circle; you can always enlarge your circle as you go if you are on the safe side. However, if you begin as if for a correct circle and your horse drifts out further, there is nothing you can do to bring him back without disturbing the regularity of rhythm and bend, something very visible to any judge sitting at C or B.

A second tip is to always start your circle from a shoulder-fore position. Never start from a straight or outside-positioned horse. Starting the circle in the shoulder-fore position reduces the difficulty of the circle by the equivalent of at least one meter because the front is already off the straight track, the horse is properly bent from the first step, and the engagement is already in place before the circle is begun.

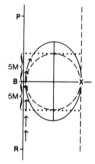

Avoiding the difficulty of a 10-meter circle. Not easy to see from C but judged insufficient from B or E.

Don't try to avoid the difficulty by riding an oval on the longitudinal axis. This is easily seen by the judge at E and B although difficult for the judge at C. It's just as insufficient a performance as exceeding the diameter over the centerline for a 10-meter circle.

The most important fact is not to approach the circle faster than the horse can handle it. Again, since the circle at E and B is often a movement shortly following your entrance, the rate and rhythm at which the horse is allowed to travel after the halt at X will determine if you can or cannot ride the circle at E or B properly. The key decision, then, is not once you are past C; the decision and determination of your success with this circle is made while you are saluting the judge and deciding at what speed and rhythm you will be riding after X.

While circles of any size are an opportunity for the good rider to put the horse into a rounder frame and improve the engagement of the inside hind leg, this is not necessarily the case with trot or canter circles ridden on the short side. While you may be perfectly capable of riding a correct 10-or 15-meter circle, it will be quite a different matter when that 10-meter circle is ridden at A or C, as in Second Level Test 2.

A good way to practice it is to make a square of 10- or 15-meters with ground poles and ride inside to give you an idea of how tight it really is.

Let's look first at the geometry and angle of vision for this movement. Ridden correctly, the circle is based at A or C, limited by the two quarter lines, and reaching a point 4 meters beyond G and D. The judge at C has a perfect angle of vision, with a clear view of the quarter lines as well as the apex of the circle at G or D. Exceeding any of these points is just as insufficient as riding over the centerline at X on a 10-meter circle at E or B. Furthermore, with the circle at A or C, you do not have the worn track of the centerline or a worn out spot at X to tell

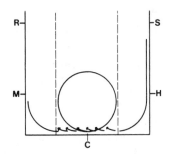

you where you are. In addition, as mentioned earlier, the hoof-prints of the preceding horses go too large in 90% of all the rides. So, again, ride your own circle and don't follow the hoofprints in the footing.

Since there are always evenly spaced sections of the enclosure, usually chains and pins, it is easy for the judge to ascertain the correct location of the quarter lines. That is exactly what you should do, too, on foot before you ride. Inspect each ring you will ride in since every ring is different depending on the number of sections on the short side. Figure out exactly where the quarter lines are and don't guess!

The Figure "S"

The figure "S" is a much more elegant way to change hands than just riding straight from E to B, as first called for in First Level Test 3. Furthermore, it is not a very difficult movement and allows you to put your horse in an excellent frame with his haunches engaged. Start the movement from riding straight on the long side, and prepare for the turn with the shoulder-fore position. In Second Level Test 3, it is even easier since you approach and finish the movement in shoulder-in.

The problem is, as always, the transition on the centerline which is exactly in view of the judge at C. What happens all too often is that when the rider and the front of the horse reach the centerline and change position, the rider forgets that the horse's hunches are still on the first circle. They end up crossing diago-

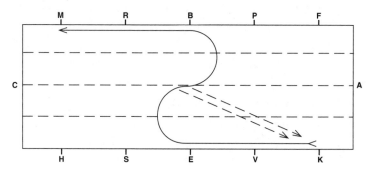

nally and never being straight on the centerline.

So, ride as if you wanted to go back to F or K and look at those letters, and not at A, before changing direction and bending your horse to the other side. Also, since you are not riding a figure eight, there is no need to be concerned with the anchor point of the movement. You need only be concerned with changing your weight from the old inside to the new inside and riding ahead of your horse.

The Serpentine

The serpentine, an apparently simple movement, is not easy to ride correctly at all. All too often I see riders just relax a little bit too much and the results are accordingly bad. Here are the basic points to keep in mind: Serpentines start and finish at A or C, so starting or finishing a serpentine in a corner is an error. This should be equal to minus 2, or if the judge is lenient, an incorrectly executed movement rated as "insufficient." This is clearly spelled out in the AHSA *Rule Book*.

A serpentine in three loops is a sequence of three 20-meter half-circles passing the same points as in a 20-meter circle: from A to four meters beyond K, returning to centerline two meters beyond L. Touch on B, return to centerline two meters before I. Reach the outside track four meters before H and return to C staying out of the corner. In order to avoid the horse sticking to the enclosure of the arena, it is better to ride the half-circles just inside of the normal track to maintain the smoothness and roundness of the half-circles. In such a serpentine there are no corners; there is no back tracking.

First Level Test 1 calls for a serpentine in trot, and in Second Level Test 2 there is a canter serpentine, both ridden from A to C.

The basics we look for in the serpentine are:

■ Rhythm. Since you are riding only sections of large circles, you must show total regularity and good, forward strides.

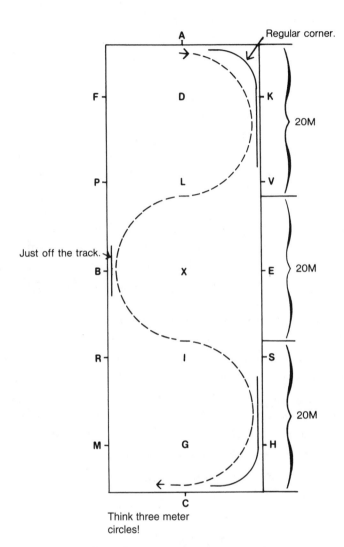

A

Regular corner.

F ⊣

D

K ⊢

20M

P ⊣

L

V ⊢

Just off the track.

B ⊣

X

E ⊢ 20M

R ⊣

I

S ⊢

20M

M ⊣

G

H ⊢

C

Think three meter
circles!

■ The precision of the movements must be correct and all semi-circles exactly of the same size. To ride a smaller half-circle to the left if the horse bends better to the left in order to have more space going to the right, avoids the difficulty of the movement and therefore must be rated as insufficient. Beware of riding into the corner or sticking to the enclosure of the arena; the consequences were mentioned before.

■ The horse must be on one track, bent correctly and equally to both sides, and must be absolutely steady on the bit
without resistance.

Leg-Yielding

The most controversial movement in the training of a young
horse is leg-yielding. There are fervent advocates and just as
many with very serious reservations. Nor is this controversy
new: it goes back to Newcastle, Steinbrecht, de la Gueriniere,
Seunig, Decarpentry, and Podhajsky, to name just a few.

It is no wonder this particular movement has been in and out
of tests since the inception of dressage competition. Currently
though, leg-yielding is in the tests again and, irrespective of how
we feel about it, we have to ride and judge it as defined in the
AHSA rules.

The movement itself is not very difficult if performed on its
own. That is, to have a practically straight horse with only a
slight bend, move away from the inside leg ,helped by the weight
of the rider ahead of the movement, preferably not falling out on
his outside shoulder or losing position and rhythm, while maintaining steadiness on the bit. What makes for the degree of difficulty is the way leg-yielding is incorporated into the test. We

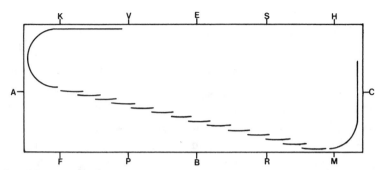

should also realize that leg-yielding does not encourage engagement but, instead, puts the horse on the forehand, particularly when executed on a straight line.

The easiest approach to leg-yielding is to come from the long side onto the centerline, maintaining the bend, and move the horse over to the other long side on a shallow diagonal, riding energetically forward and softly sideways. The keys to a good leg-yielding are balance, rhythm, and position of the horse.

The leg-yielding required in First Level Test 2 is much easier to ride than those requested in previous tests. The movements flow very naturally. And, since the movement begins from the centerline at D, there is ample room to be prepared. A slight shift of weight to the outside (look where you go), plus the inside leg in the rhythm of the inside diagonal (right hind leg), on a practically straight horse will give you a fluid, balanced movement. The enclosure of the ring will bring your leg-yielding to an end without you having to do anything about it. Just bring your inside shoulder back, shift your weight back to the inside by looking in the direction you are traveling.

THE WALK AND WALK MOVEMENTS

The walk is one of the most difficult gaits, and the gait that is worked on properly the least. And, if the walk is practiced, it is usually done in such a way that the basic gait is ruined.

The walk is also a dead giveaway of the education the horse has received and the level of knowledge and experience of the rider or instructor. While we see many nice medium walks in the lower levels, they become progressively more rare. Pacing, or a tendency to pace, lack of extension, and/or irregularities of rhythm become almost the rule as horses are trained for the higher levels.

Once ruined, it is almost impossible for the average rider to regain a correct walk. Since a dressage horse is required to have three correct gaits, one can hardly expect sufficient collective marks for gaits if only the canter and trot are acceptable. But let's not forget that horses generally have correct gaits before they are trained, and they should maintain correct gaits while they are being progressively educated.

Judges are happy to see a good forward walk, on the bit, in correct rhythm, covering ground, and with the ability to go on a long rein, with a smooth transition back onto the bit with shorter rein without showing any change in the basic pace. The key for a good walk is simply forward, forward, forward. Restraining or shortening the gait with rein aids, particularly in the lower levels, is the beginning of the end for a decent walk.

There is often confusion regarding the difference between the working and medium walk. Let's look at and compare the old *Rule Book's* definitions of each:

WORKING WALK	MEDIUM WALK
■ A regular and unconstrained walk.	■ A free, regular and unconstrained walk of moderate extension.
■ The rider should maintain a light and steady contact with the horse's mouth.	■ The rider maintains a light but steady contact with the mouth.
■ The horse should walk energetically but calmly and determined steps with distinctly marked four equally spaced beats.	■ The horse remaining on the bit walks energetically but calmly with even and determined steps, the hind feet touching the ground in front of the footprints of the fore feet feet.

So, there is really little difference between the working walk and the medium walk. If you have a nice working walk with a clear overstride, it is a medium walk. If you can put your horse in a slightly rounder frame from behind and make it look more elegant, fine. But don't try to tamper with the rhythm or length of stride. Remember, it's best to leave the walk alone!

However, due to this similarity of definitions of working and medium walk and following the international standard, working walk has been eliminated from the current tests; there is only medium walk. Free walk is left in the tests up to Second Level. Extended walk begins at Third Level, and collected walk at Fourth Level. This is to preserve the purity of the gait and make any gait "manipulation" unnecessary.

The other walk that must be shown in the lower levels is a free walk on long rein. A long rein does not mean loose. The horse should stretch and it is not necessary to keep the poll at the highest point.

In the free walk, there are three basic things you must show the judge. First, the overstride, rhythm and desire to move forward should be the same as in the medium walk. Then, the horse should stretch forward when allowed to do so. And, the horse should come back to the shorter frame and acceptance of the bit in the transition from free walk to medium walk without resistance, or a change in stride or rhythm.

Many old masters suggest not attempting any shortening or collection of the walk before the horse is fully confirmed in collected canter and collected trot, something which is not achieved before Fourth Level or Prix St. George. In addition, by those levels the rider should be sufficiently advanced to not only feel the proper footfalls but to be able to influence the rhythm and regularity with his aids, certainly something which no young or inexperienced rider can do.

If you need to make a decision to show or not show a certain type of walk required in a test, my personal decision would be to never force a walk on my horse for which he is not ready. I would rather accept an insufficient mark from the judge. Judges change and tests change, but once you have ruined the walk of your horse, that is unlikely to change!

Experience also suggests that not all types of horses react the same to improper training in the walk. European Warmbloods are frustratingly sensitive to developing trouble with the rhythm and pacing, while Arabian and related breeds seem to be at the other end of the scale. But each rider must judge his own horse or, even better, have someone knowledgeable as the ground man to watch in training.

THE TURN ON THE HAUNCHES

A good definition is in the AHSA *Rule Book:*

"The horse's forehand moves in even, quiet and regular steps

around the horse's inner hindleg while maintaining the rhythm

of the walk. In the half turn on the haunches the horse is not

required to step with its inside hind leg in the same spot each

time it leaves the ground but may move slightly forward.

Backing or loss of rhythm are considered a serious fault. This

movement may be executed through 90 degrees, 180 degrees, or

360 degrees."

As first called for in Second Level, judges are looking for two basic points in the turn on the haunches: first, the regularity of the rhythm in the walk, leading to a turn around the haunches with all four legs maintaining the normal footfall; and, second, a properly bent horse, who remains bent in the direction he is moving while staying on the outside rein.

This sounds very easy and it can be, provided you do not try too hard. Remember that the turn on the haunches is a variation of the forward motion; it is not a lateral movement. It is not to be ridden from a slowed down walk.

What I see too often is a fair or poor medium walk, or even a collected walk, with or without a tendency to pace. And when coming closer to the movement, the rider further interferes by slowing down. Pacing becomes evident, the regularity of the rhythm is lost, and the horse becomes disorganized in his movement, or "stuck." As a result, the turn is not a regular step-by-step movement. The hind legs get stuck and lose their impulsion, or the horse pivots on his inside hind leg. The horse leans on the bit or gets above it, and loses the bend. The rider sits on the outside while giving absolutely no support with his seat or legs. Once this disaster is terminated, it takes the horse at least two to five steps to regain some semblance of balance before having to repeat the same maneuver to the other side. In addition, stepping out, stepping back or turning in the middle will lead to insufficient scores.

Looking at it as a judge from any letter on the arena, the slightest mistake is only too visible, no matter from which angle one looks at the performance. The rider should be perfectly aware that, unlike some movements, there is absolutely nothing he can hide in the turn on the haunches.

The turn on the haunches and later, the pirouette, are movements of precision and technical correctness that reflect primarily the competence of the rider and, to a much lesser degree, the training and ability of the horse. The performance of the turn on the haunches or the pirouette will therefore not only affect the mark for the movement itself, but will also influence the collected marks for the rider, reflecting on his ability and the correct use of the aids.

Young horses are not completely symmetrical in their ability to turn to the right and to the left. One regularly sees good turns to one side and poor turns to the other side by horses lacking equal suppleness. However, it is in these circumstances that the aids the rider uses demonstrate his ability and skill. It is certainly better to make a wider turn in a forward movement than make it too small and get stuck, losing regularity of rhythm and balance.

Also, in competition it is essential to show an identical turn to the left and right. Many judges wait to see both turns before giving their marks, and reward equality but punish unequal performances. Therefore, the key to equal turns is to adjust the better side to the ability of the poorer side.

The most frequent basic mistakes I see in the turn on the haunches are:

■ A slowing down or restraining of the walk when approaching the turn.

■ The rider sitting to the outside of the movement instead of the inside.

■ Total inactivity of the inside supporting leg of the rider. This aid is essential to keep the horse's inside leg moving forward and under against the restraining outside rein. To facilitate this coordination, the movement can be started from a shoulder-fore position in a very active and animated working walk.

THE REIN BACK

Backing a few steps is another dead giveaway of the ability of the rider, much more so than that of the horse. Since the rein back in Second Level is always done at A or C, the judge at C has an absolutely perfect view.

The evaluation for the rein back encompasses a series of elements and the rider must be very conscious that they all contribute to the total score, not just the few steps backward.

Analyzing the movement we have:

■ The down transition from the trot which must come from behind with the horse remaining light on the bit and in front of the rider's legs with no walk steps before the halt.

■ The halt itself: square in front and back, exactly on the centerline at A or C (not before and not after), with the haunches under the horse and not strung out behind. The horse must remain on the bit.

- The preparation for the rein back: never rushed, and practically invisible except by watching the body language of the horse such as the ears, tail, arching of the neck, and so on.

- The rein back itself: performed with a minimum of aids, but definitely not using the reins as a means to pull the horse back.

- The backward steps must be diagonal, coordinated, quiet, rhythmic and free. This is instantly followed by the forward transition, using the hind leg that took the last step back to engage the forward movement.

So, the quality of the rein back is not only determined by the number of steps but by the ease, proper coordination, absence of any resistance, and smoothness of the transitions, while maintaining regularity in the walk, rhythm with the proper frame, acceptance of the bit, and engagement throughout the movement.

What is the key to a good rein back? In my opinion, it is a progressive and deliberate preparation of the horse on the long side, or during the preceding movement, in order to arrive at an engaged halt. Try to maintain a steady rhythm, with no rushing, and avoiding the tendency of the horse to fall on the forehand. This will result in the type of halt from which any horse can rein back lightly and elegantly with the correct transition forward, either to a walk, a trot or a canter once the rein back has been completed.

If the horse rein backs from a poor halt on the forehand into a position that does not allow for an instant forward transition to any of the three gaits, the rein back was done incorrectly. Therefore, a good observer can predict from the way the rider prepares his horse preceding the halt if he will succeed or not. Remember, the rein back is much more a test of the rider than the horse.

The most common mistakes in the rein back are:

- Insufficient preparation by the rider.

- A halt done before the centerline (eight out of ten horses do that).

■ The horse must remain in front of the rider's leg throughout the movement.

■ The rider pulling the horse back with the reins while driving forward with the seat and legs.

■ Resistance in the rein back leading to lack of the backward steps, and a leaning on the bit, with a dropping of the front end.

■ A poor transition forward without balance and with hesitation.

■ The rider does not take the necessary time to proceed deliberately from one stage to the next.

I have not spoken about the number of steps to be taken because, in my opinion, this is secondary to the quality of the execution of the movement in the lower levels.

THE CANTER AND CANTER MOVEMENTS

The real range of canter work doesn't start until Third Level, so we will not discuss it here extensively except to refer to the very fundamental requirements for the lower levels. Based on the fact that demanding canter work comes much later in training, the lower level tests are similarly much less demanding in the canter requirements than for the trot. We are looking for only very basic and simple movements, such as working canter, cantering on straight lines, a few circles, and transitions in and out of the trot. In Second Level, canter from the walk and counter-canter are required.

The key to good marks is in the transitions into the canter; they determine the quality of the gait. A horse that does not remain on the bit will throw his head or rush, and usually ends up crooked, unbalanced, and on the forehand. This makes the canter depart, as well as the subsequent movement, insufficient. To rebalance, straighten, and re-establish a correct canter is just not possible under competitive conditions with a young or inexperienced horse.

On the other hand, if the transition has been correct, the ensuing flowing working canter is a relief for the horse's back from the sitting trot and very pleasant to watch as well as to ride. Very often I see young horses unsteady on the bit, with a hollow and stiff back in the sitting trot, suddenly going relaxed with a low neck, on the bit and a supple working back in the canter. This is a giveaway that the horse has not yet developed a sufficiently strong back to take the demands of the sitting trot. A similar problem is often observed in the transition from a rising trot to a sitting trot.

The same basic quality of gaits applies to the canter as to the trot: regularity of rhythm, acceptance of the bit, straightness, engagement, desire to move forward, ability to bend, and so on. To secure these qualities, it is best to ride the canter in a slight shoulder-fore position, and to develop the canter with very light half halts with the inside seat and leg against a steady outside rein and a giving inside hand. The success of canter is always in the transition. It is much more important to work on the transition from the walk or trot into the proper canter than to just keep on cantering on and on. Once cantering, you must allow the movement with a giving inside hand in the rhythm of the gait.

In the transition from the canter to the trot, you should still consider this a forward transition; it should be a transition into a forward, energetic trot. It is definitely not a progressive cranking down of a forward canter into a creeping, unrhythmic trot, achieved by pulling on the reins.

It is essential that these simple canter transitions be mastered before attempting to show at a level where a change of lead through the trot is required. Unless the down transition to the trot comes from behind, how can the horse properly strike out on the other lead from behind, still light on the bit, balanced, bent correctly and in front of the rider's leg?

What further complicates the canter-trot-canter movement is that it has to be done to both sides, and performed in an identical fashion both times. The number of trot steps taken is therefore determined by the difficult side. Showing three trot steps in one transition and five in the other only proves to the judge that the rider does not control the movement, or that the horse is not yet capable of doing it identically to both sides. This certainly does not rate much more than a satisfactory mark of 5. Also, anything beyond five trot steps is too much. In addition, the change of lead through the trot must be straight, forward, effortless, balanced, equal to both sides, and performed exactly at X in order to be considered more than just acceptable.

THE TROT-CANTER TRANSITION IN THE CORNER AND ITS CONSEQUENCES

In the lower level tests, we have a transition at C or A from a walk to the trot, and then at M, H, F or K, the canter depart. This should be a simple movement where one can pick up a good score. Unfortunately, it is most often executed in a way that hardly rates a 5 and also ruins the movements that follow.

What usually happens is that the rider begins to canter before the horse has completed the turn and straightened. Further, if the rider uses the outside leg as the aid to canter on instead of the inside aids against the outside rein, the horse's haunches fall even further to the inside. The inside hind leg, instead of stepping under the horse, moves laterally on a third track. Such transitions don't rate very much and speak rather poorly of the rider's skill.

This kind of transition is extremely difficult to correct on the long side. It contributes to a poor mark for the next movement, too, since the horse is crooked, with his haunches falling in. Further, the rider puts himself in an even worse predicament if he has to ride a 15-meter circle at B or E as required at First Level. As a matter of fact, on a young horse it is impossible to ride a 15-meter circle if the horse is positioned to the outside and crooked. In beginning the circle, the poor horse is either thrown off balance with the inside rein, or exceeds the centerline by one to three meters. This is a totally insufficient performance and will result in a 4 for the canter transition and a 3 or 4 for the circle. It has nothing to do with the horse, but is entirely the fault of the rider: his poor planning and the lack of understanding of what is expected of him. It is also a typical example of how an incorrectly ridden movement perpetuates itself in the next one and so on.

So how should one ride the transition to canter after the corner?

■ Prepare the transition into the trot at A or C with light half halts so that the horse stays in front of your legs, with his hind quarters coming under.

■ Choose a moderate speed; there is a corner ahead. Ride the corner as part of a 10-meter circle, properly bent and in good rhythm.

■ At F, hold the bend, being certain that the horse is straight on the long side and in a slight shoulder-fore position.

■ Ask for the canter by mainly using your inside aids against your outside rein in order to be sure the inside hind leg steps properly under the horse. Keep the bend down the long side until B or until the next movement.

As a result, the horse will be straight and under himself, engaged, and you can hold the shoulder-fore position as long as you want. You will have a horse correctly bent, on the bit, engaged, and can ride any circle you want, or any other move-

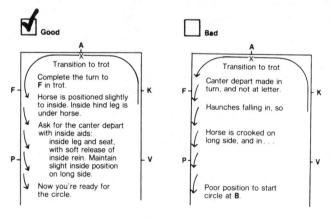

The Canter Depart

ment required.

Remember, it is just as easy to ride this movement correctly as incorrectly and you may easily get a 6 or an 8 as a score instead of a 3 or 4.

I believe that it is better in the lower levels to ride with the slight position to the inside along the straight long sides. Later, when we reach Second or Third Levels and above, the horse will be required to be perfectly straight on the outside rein.

The importance of having a properly positioned horse in the canter becomes particularly important in the lengthening of the stride and in the medium and extended canter. A horse can only make a proper down transition in a few strides if his hind legs are under him and not laterally placed. Otherwise, he has no way of braking and will fall on the forehand and barrel through the corner. Therefore, one should teach the horse to canter in a slight shoulder-fore position at the beginning of his training when asking for a lengthening or medium canter. This will ensure that when the transition comes at the end of the long side, the horse is truly under himself with some self-carriage and straight.

COUNTER-CANTER

First introduced in Second Level, counter-canter ("False Canter") is a test of balance, self-carriage and sustained engagement. In higher levels, counter-canter is performed in serpentines combined with flying changes. In Second Level, though, what we are asked for is that the horse execute a half-circle or a corner on the outside lead in a well collected frame.

The basic criteria for counter-canter are:

■ The horse should be consistently on the bit and collected.

■ The same rhythm should be maintained throughout the movements.

■ Self-carriage and engagement should be maintained, resulting in lightness of the front.

■ The horse should be slightly flexed to the outside.

- The movement is always on one track.
- A correct three-beat canter is maintained.

Some usual faults are:

- The horse's frame getting longer, losing the engagement.
- Going faster or slower than in the true canter.
- The horse progressively falling on the forehand, leaning on the bit.
- The horse overflexed on the inside rein.
- The haunches falling out.
- A four-beat canter.

So what is the requirement for riding a decent counter-canter? As noted, the quality of the preceding simple change, with both transitions from and to the canter coming from behind on an engaged and balanced horse is the first requirement. In addition, effective half halts ridden from your seat (not hands) must be used as needed to maintain this frame and self-carriage. In the early stages of counter-canter, let the horse do the job; don't be over demanding. Soften your inside hand. This will help to maintain a correct footfall, but the horse will be a little more on the

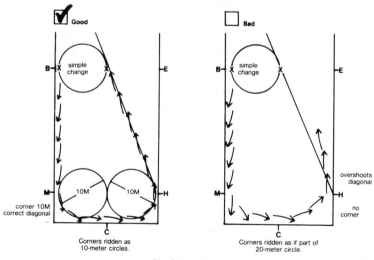

The Counter-Canter Options

forehand. This is another case where any defect in training, even minor ones, becomes an instantly glaring short-coming. There is just no way to bluff your way through this technical movement.

Enhancing the difficulty, the counter-canter includes straight lines and two corners. One option you have is to ride a 20-meter half-circle and make it as easy on your horse as possible. The more secure in the movement your horse is, the more you can approach the ideal of going straight, riding the corner, going straight, riding the corner, and again straight. Note that attempting a 6-meter volte-type corner at this level of training is unrealistic, but a 10-meter corner should certainly be rated as "good."

But what is more important, the quality of the gait or the corners? There is no question that the quality of the gait is more important, but with all things being equal, the horse with the better corner gets the higher score. However, a four-beat counter-canter, on the forehand with haunches out of control, is only a 4 or less, no matter how deeply the corner is ridden.

THE SIMPLE CHANGE

The simple change, canter to walk to canter, is introduced in Second Level 3 and 4. The *Rule Book* states:

"This is a change of leg where the horse is brought back into the walk and, after at the most three steps, is restarted into a canter with the other leg leading with no steps at the trot."

This is a test to see if your horse is capable of collection, combined with proper transitions, originating from the hind quarters. If you cannot ride the simple change blindfolded, you are not ready for Third Level.

The fact that you may be by now riding flying changes to both sides is no reason to forget the simple change. In Second Level, simple changes are made as easy as possible: the approach is not straight but on a circle, a basic condition that helps to engage the inside hind leg for the down transition. Only if this transition is correct will the canter depart be correct on the other lead.

If you succeed in a canter-walk transition, but fall on the forehand in the process, your canter depart will be made through the trot and your score less than 5. So, the key to success is in the proper preparation in the approach to this difficult transition.

The simple change is also a test of whether or not you have achieved longitudinal suppleness and self-carriage in your horse. It also tests if you, the rider, are sufficiently proficient to sustain collection through two rapidly succeeding transitions.

STRETCHING THE FRAME (CHEWING THE REINS OUT OF THE HANDS)

The 1995 tests at Training and First Level include a new movement that is much misunderstood. Performed in rising trot on a 20-meter circle, the movement calls for "letting the horse gradually chew the reins out of the hands," then, "gradually take up the reins." The horse should stretch forward and down with a light contact, while maintaining his balance, rhythm and the quality of the gait.

This has absolutely nothing to do with giving the horse a loose rein as when work is finished, or when a tense horse pulls the reins out of the hands of the rider.

Instead, it is executed by opening the fingers, including the grip between the thumb and index finger, allowing the horse to stretch down while maintaining an even and consistent contact. During this movement, the muscles of the crest relax, along with the muscles of the jaw. The weight of the head and neck pull them down, stretching the ligaments in the back from the head to the tail. It is the stretching of these muscles and ligaments connecting the base of the tongue to the chest and shoulder blades that induce the horse to "chew," relaxing the lower jaw. This is reflected in the entire horse, not just in the upper neck and shoulder.

When performed correctly, this movement is exactly the opposite of "taking" the reins out of the hand. In taking the reins out of the hands, the muscles of the neck tighten up, the mastoidal muscle closes the mouth tightly, setting the jaw. The occipital muscles pull the head forward and in doing so, tensing the entire horse. In that case, pulling the reins out of the hands of the rider is mostly a defensive movement by the horse against poor hands.

The correct "chewing of the reins out of the hand" takes place only if the horse has confidence in the rider's hands—which means there must be good hands based on a correct seat.

In doing so, the angle between the head and neck remains more or less the same and consequently the nose goes behind the vertical the more the horse stretches down. This is also the basis of the "long and low" concept in warming up, to relax the neck and back muscles of the horse. While long popular in Germany, the movement is becoming more so by knowledgeable riders in the U.S. for its supreme benefits.

Since the movement stretches the back muscles and ligaments of the horse's spine, the back comes up, almost arching like a cat, and starts swinging. The horse just taking the reins from the rider or the rider just dropping the reins does not stretch these muscles and ligaments and, as a result, the back drops and the entire objective of the movement is negated. While this exercise can be executed in the walk, trot, and canter, in the 1995 tests it is asked for in the most simple way: rising trot on a 20-meter circle.

In addition to the correct release of the reins, an equally important aspect is to ride the horse energetically forward. Riding on a 20-meter circle obviously helps to maintain the inside hind leg under the horse, and moving forward can be further encouraged by posting on the "wrong" diagonal. This puts the rider down in the saddle and leg on the horse's side as his inside hind leg is in the air and in the process of reaching forward.

A light seat is essential during this movement and it is a good thing it is executed in rising trot; the last thing we want to do with a young horse at this stage of training is push his back down! Therefore, the upper body of the rider should also relax, and even bend a little bit forward in the direction of the stretch.

The proof that the horse has really accepted the bit and has confidence in the rider's hands is the last phase of this movement, the reestablishing of the original frame. This is best done by sitting slightly straighter up, shortening both reins with one hand, and reestablishing the original rein contact with the other hand in a soft, consistent movement. This is done while urging the horse forward from the inside leg, without allowing any change in rhythm, tempo, or forwardness.

What we as judges don't want to see is a horse that does not stretch forward and down, or that jerks on the reins. He should not change his rhythm or tempo, or fall on the forehand. He must not just lower his neck, while avoiding stretching to the bit. And, needless to say, the geometry of the circle must be maintained–no drifting in or out.

This movement is, once again, a clear indication of correct training and development of the horse; a well-trained horse stretches better than a youngster. It is not intended as a "parlor trick!"

UBERSTREICHEN

The 1995 tests, beginning with Second Level 1, call for a movement known commonly by the German term *ubertsreichen:* the clear release of inside rein or both reins. It is the final exercise to demonstrate that the horse and rider have mastered the basic aids of rein, seat, and leg coordination, leading to a horse in total self-carriage and a rider in harmony with his mount.

In this Second Level movement, the inside hand reaches halfway up the crest, slowly and steadily, for three to four strides, while the contact with the outside rein is maintained. The inside hand then returns to its initial position in a soft, slow movement, reestablishing the contact without ripping the horse in the mouth.

Second Level Test 1 requires this movement to be performed at the canter on a 20-meter circle. The Directive Ideas on the movement give the clear idea of what is being sought: "Clear release of contact where the horse maintains self-carriage, rhythm, bend and quality of the canter."

Later, in Third Level, the movement is performed on a straight line with both hands extended up the horse's neck.

I think it is worth a reminder here that the frame of the horse, including the position of the neck and head, are conditioned by the engagement and thrust created by the haunches (impulsion and collection). We ride the horse back to front; through the back into our hands and never the other way around. When this is correct, this clear release of the reins should have no repercussions on the quality of the movement.

An incorrectly trained or ridden horse will take advantage of the release, and fall on the forehand, change the bend, change the tempo, or lose self-carriage or balance.

It's also worth noting that *uberstreichen* should be a routine check for the rider during schooling, clear up to Grand Prix, and not just a movement for competition.

The Last Problem: The Diagonal to the Centerline

Almost all tests finish from the diagonal onto the centerline, with the final halt and salute at X. But don't relax too soon! You are not yet home when you start the diagonal and, in the lower levels, this is one of the most difficult sequences of movements to ride correctly.

It is not the movement, but the transition into a safe and steady turn onto the centerline that increases the difficulty and tests the horse and rider for the last time before leaving the ring.

The problems at Training Level are very different from those found later, so let's look at them first.

A 10-meter circle cannot be ridden on a horse that's going too forward in a working gait, and who is just learning to bend and remain on the contact. Therefore, don't speed up on the preceding movement. Keep the rhythm and balance and, if anything, ride more conservatively, using half halts and solid support on

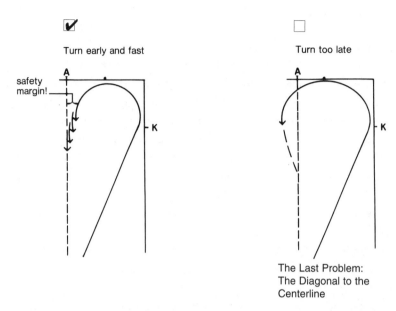

Turn early and fast

Turn too late

safety margin!

The Last Problem:
The Diagonal to the
Centerline

the approach. Position your horse to the left before reaching F or K and start turning immediately once you get there.

Above all, do not look at A; you are not supposed to go there anyway. Instead, look at D, which you must hit dead on. It is very much like jumping a tight hunter course: if you don't look at your next fence, you will miss the turn. Turn as much as you can early on, easing off in the second half of the turn, in order to maintain the rhythm and impulsion, and aim for two feet inside the centerline. If your horse drifts, you are still safe. If you are steady on the turn, ease off a bit and let your horse drift a little. Use more inside leg to keep the impulsion and go forward on the centerline.

This final movement is not only a test for your horse, but to see if you know how to ride smart.

By the time you move up to First and Second Levels, you must have mastered the simple turn from a working trot. Here the problem is much different, since it is impossible to ride a three-quarter 10-meter circle in a lengthened or medium trot. The key is, as usual, the down transition to a working or collected trot

from the preceeding movement, in most First and Second Level
tests a diagonal.

At this stage of training, this down transition requires at least
three to four strides, but the text of the test says the movement
goes from M to K. Depending on your ability to lengthen and
come back, you have a series of options. The difficulties you
meet at K are proportional to the ability of your horse to length-
en: the better the lengthening or medium trot, the bigger the
problem. The ideal would be to ride the lengthening full out from
M to K, make a one stride transition down, and then ride the turn
as described earlier for Training Level.

However, you hardly ever see this, even at the Grand Prix
Level, because of the difficulty. Top scores are hard to get for
diagonals, since both transitions—in and out—count. If one of
them is not done correctly, it is impossible to get an 8 on the
movement.

So, what are your options on this movement?

■ You can compromise a bit on your lengthening, medium
or extended trot, by not going all out so that you can ride a
smoother transition at K. This will lower your score, though,
because it is evident if a horse gives the maximum or not on
the diagonal.

■ You can go all out from M to X and then gradually slow
down, starting your down transition halfway between X and
K. This is safe, but an unsatisfactory situation and easily
spotted by the judge and scored accordingly.

So what is the solution?

Compromise on precision. Go to the track two or three meters
before K, and ride your down transition with a solid half halt on
the outside and your back to the judge. Use the two or three
strides you've gained on the track to bring your horse down, bend
to the inside, and move into the corner collected, engaged, and
balanced.

Considering the angle of vision from C, this is probably the
best solution to this problem, but don't expect an automatic 7 or

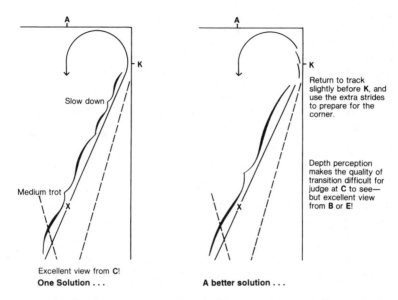

One Solution . . .   **A better solution . . .**

8 since the final transition, when ridden as above, still avoids the true difficulty asked for in the test.

This is the solution you see most often, though, up to and including FEI levels. Even a proficient rider feels it is better to get a 7 for the final diagonal by compromising the precision of the final down transition, but still having a good chance for an 8 on the centerline and the final salute. So, don't blame the judge, who can't appreciate just your superb diagonal; he's required to look for more than that: your transition, turn and centerline.

The solution taken by many beginners is to ride straight into the corner, expecting the horse to make a roll-back in balance and rhythm, and finish, by magic, somehow at X. This certainly would be a feat that deserves a 10, or maybe even more, if it could be performed successfully!

Another problem you might expect is that, as we said before, A is rarely in the middle of the ring. This affects not only your entry in the beginning of the test, but your strategy in the end. Let's assume A is closer to the corner at K by three or four feet (not unusual) that the geometrically true centerline. This makes your final turn even more difficult because it is now close to an

8 meter three-quarter circle—very hard for a Training Level horse.

In these cases, you must be very conservative in your approach. Even in the more advanced levels, your down transition from a lengthening or extended trot must be perfect. There is no way you can barrel through the corner and finish by sheer luck on the centerline when coming from a medium or extended trot.

On the other hand, if A is closer to F, you are really lucky. You can give it all you have for the last movement since your turn to the centerline will be larger than 10 meters. In this case, you should just say thank you to the volunteers who put up the ring!

In conclusion, then, if your test is only five to seven minutes of actual riding, there is no such thing as an easy ending like the last jump on a cross-country course. Beware of the test designers—they will not give you a chance to fall asleep! Instead, they put many hidden difficulties in the test to ascertain if you have really done a solid basic training program and if you can choose intelligent alternatives suitable to your horse.

CHAPTER SIX:

THE SUPPLEMENTAL AIDS AND WHEN TO USE THEM

THE definition of dressage states that the training of the horse should make him light, obedient, and responsive to the slightest aids of the rider. Therefore, the better the horse, the less we need forceful and obvious commands. We should be able to ride the test requirements with minimal aids such as seat, legs, position, distribution of weight, and very quiet hands.

You may argue that it is mandatory at FEI levels to wear spurs and ride in a double bridle. Admittedly that's true, but any properly schooled Grand Prix horse can easily perform in a snaffle without the rider using any spurs or a whip. The requirement for spurs and double bridle traces back to the days of the Cavalry and the actual use of horses in battle, when total control of the horse was a matter of life and death. In addition, riding had to be done with the left hand only (the weapon being held in the right), and under very difficult conditions.

Today, the requirement to wear spurs and use a double bridle at the FEI level is more an added difficulty rather than an asset for most riders. An incorrect leg position frequently leads to interference with spurs. An improperly adjusted curb often leads to an instantaneous negative reaction by the horse. Both can lead to a reduction in the collective marks for the rider, as well as for the score of the individual movement.

Now let's consider each of the supplemental aids.

THE SPURS

Spurs used range from inoffensive little stubs to a three-inch daggers, with or without sharp rollers. I have even seen spurs having sharp spikes and rollers on the inside shank, which is more related to cruelty to animals than to proper riding. In my opinion, using such devices should be grounds for being thrown out of the ring! Spurs should be more decorative, and a sign of a proper leg position under all circumstances. With a poor rider, they are a dead giveaway of faulty leg position.

Regrettably, spurs are worn today beginning in Training Level. Fundamentally, I believe the same consideration should apply to spurs as the double bridle: they should only be allowed at Fourth Level and above. Uneducated legs should not be armed with spurs, just as uneducated riders with poor hands are not allowed to ride with a double bridle until they are sufficiently proficient to perform at Fourth Level or above. Let's face it, in the lower levels the size and aggressiveness of the spurs is directly proportional to the incompetence of the rider.

While riding has made enormous progress in the U.S. as far as seat and hands are concerned, a proper and consistent leg position is still a rarity with most riders, even in the FEI levels. If you scrutinize the pictures of winning dressage competitors, you see immediately that more often than not, toes are out and spurs are in, even at the halt. Some riders even seem to expect the horse to do a decent half-pass while moving vigorously and evenly against their inside spur, without realizing what they are doing. This is certainly not a sight to impress the judge with the rider's ability.

The worst is when spurs are deliberately used to drive a horse against unreasonable restraints by the reins, especially when a lot of curb rein action is used in the hope that some kind of a frame or collection can be forced on the poor animal. This is neither a pretty picture nor does it deserve any good marks.

For beginners and lower level riders, who don't know where their legs are or when and how to use the spurs correctly, it's better to leave the spurs in the tackroom!

THE WHIP

Carrying a whip is allowed in all national levels and some international tests, with the exception of finals competitions and FEI Level tests. But let's not forget that good tests can be ridden without it, and have been for a long time. If a rider wants to carry a whip, he should certainly do so correctly, by having it on the side he anticipates having to use it.

To be allowed a whip in regular competition and not in the finals makes absolutely no sense to me. There are scores of unfortunate riders who work their way up to the finals and then trot into the ring with the whip, only to be eliminated before they even start the test. Better get used to riding without it from the start! Also, the whip should be nothing else but the extension of your hand (if you want a third hand) or of our leg, to support the horse when needed, but never used as an instrument of punishment.

What is the judge to make of the rider who simply sits there, carrying a whip and lets problems happen without even trying to correct them? Even worse is carrying the whip on the wrong side of the horse, opposite from where he has problems.

Many professional and competitive riders complain that their horse only works correctly in the ring with a whip. However, if a horse only performs under duress with a whip in the warm-up area, and fails to perform in the ring without one, there is something fundamentally wrong with the horse's training. If this shows up in the competition, it is only fair that the horse and rider be marked down in comparison to a horse that performs well without being threatened with a whip. Let's face it, the ring is not a schooling arena.

So, I suggest that if you want to use a whip to reinforce your leg aid, know why you do it, what you want this aid for, how to carry it and use it properly. Otherwise it may cost you points throughout the test and will definitely cost you in the collective marks for the rider.

BALANCE, WEIGHT, AND THE CENTER OF GRAVITY

The combination of balance and weight is probably the most sophisticated aid when used properly. If not understood by the rider, it can severely handicap the horse in executing what we want him to perform.

All animals, as well as humans, have an acute sense of equilibrium, which is instrumental in maintaining balance and posture and, when disturbed, will be corrected instantaneously by automatic reactions.

All creatures try to keep their center of gravity as constant as possible. In the horse, the center of gravity is approximately the area under the saddle in the middle of the barrel. When a rider is added, the total weight distribution can be changed; how it is changed depends on whether or not the rider leans to the left or to the right, or forwards and backwards. With the weight of the rider, the horse's center of gravity can be altered, which in turn can trigger a reaction by the horse to correct this change.

To understand this better, think of hiking with a heavy back pack. The pack is well-balanced on your back and quite comfortable. A friend behind plays a joke and lifts the pack while at the same time he shifts it to the left and lets it down. The moment this happens, you automatically step to the left to get back under the pack in order not to fall, reestablishing a comfortable balance. You have put the center of gravity back where it belongs.

Since a horse is just as concerned with his balance and safety as a person is, he will put the rider where it's most comfortable to carry him. All horses, especially young ones, are crooked. If, for example, a horse is hollow to the left, then he will sit the rider slightly to the left of center and vice versa. Similarly, when trotting, the horse will automatically put the rider on the diagonal the horse likes better, so one ends up sitting slightly to the left, where the horse's center of gravity is located.

It is an objective of the horse's early training to develop straightness, and in doing so, placing the center of gravity truly onto the center of the horse. It takes a much experienced rider to accomplish this, one who is completely aware of where he is in relation to the horse. Riders with no balance combined with crooked horses will have a difficult time in being successful in dressage until this concept is mastered.

Once straightness has been accomplished, the center of gravity of horse and rider can be used as an aid, based on the principle that the horse is moving toward it, trying to get the center of gravity back into its natural place in order to be comfortable.

It is well known that when we sit to the right, the horse turns to the right, and when we sit to the left, the horse turns to the left. So, by shifting our seat slightly, we can influence the direction of movement on a circle or on a straight line, which reduces or obviates the need of more crude aids, such as spurs, reins, whip, etc.

On a well-trained horse, putting more weight into one stirrup and sitting slightly to one side is often enough to ride a half-pass. Like a famous European said recently, one pulls the horse after oneself in the lateral movement, such as in the half-pass or pirouette, by being ahead of the movement.

Unfortunately, this is much easier said than done. I consistently see horses executing nice bending and lateral movements to one side with a correctly positioned rider, but everything falls apart to the other side, with the rider hanging on the outside, trying to kick his horse in the other direction, and pulling on the inside rein. A sad picture indeed.

From early training up to the FEI levels, you should be very conscious of your position on the horse and how your horse is affected by this. Make sure that the combined centers of gravity (horse and rider) are a constructive aid, and not a terrible interference and handicap to the horse.

It is this very refined aid that ultimately gives a test the aspect of an effortless, balanced performance, executed without any visible aids of the rider.

Let's face it. Most of our influences on the horse are crude and based on inflicting pain on the animal in one way or another—steel bits in the mouth, double bridles, spurs, whips, etc.—expecting that the avoidance and reaction to pain leads to what we originally wanted. Isn't it time to strive to ride with true aids? Maybe dressage is a way to learn a less primitive approach to riding a horse properly.

CHAPTER SEVEN:

ANALYZING A TEST

Analyzing a test that you are considering for competition is best done at home in an easy chair, at the swimming pool, under an apple tree, or while commuting to your job (provided you don't drive).

It is not done on horseback. Practicing figures and movements and grinding your and your horse's nerves to a pulp in the dressage ring won't help.

If you understand the problems that go along with it, riding a dressage test is simply putting your intellectual assessment into actual practice. This includes choices from all options open to you, based on your horse and your own ability.

The strategy used will vary, according to different factors. These include: big horses versus small horses; well trained or not-so-well trained horses; equal or unequal suppleness to both sides; down transitions on the forehand or coming from behind, and so on. This is where your decision must come in, including how to warm up the horse (which will be discussed later). Let's go ahead now and analyze a test.

OLD AND NEW MOVEMENTS

At least 60 percent of all movements and transitions in a test have already been asked for in preceeding tests and levels. You should have no difficulty with them, provided you have spent the time needed to learn them properly when they first appeared. If you have not learned these movements, you will pay a higher and higher price for this omission as you move up the scale. When something new shows up, make sure you understand it. Remember, it is not your horse's problem; it is your responsibility to learn it correctly.

When considering moving up a test (or two), make a direct comparision with the test you have been riding. Learn what movements are new, where the coefficients are, as well as which movements repeat what you have already ridden in competition. Don't just take a chance, but instead be perfectly aware of what awaits you by thinking and planning ahead.

TECHNICAL MOVEMENTS VERSUS GAITS

When analyzing a test, you will see that there are two basic types of movements to separate and differentiate between: the technical movements and the movements of gaits.

Technical movements are those that require the skill of the rider as well as proper training of the horse. You cannot bluff your way through these movements just because your horse has good gaits.

These movements are:

- The centerline
- Halts and transitions
- The turn at C
- The turn onto the centerline
- The rein back
- The turn on the haunches or the pirouette
- The counter-canter
- Simple changes in the canter
- Changes through three steps of the trot

- Travers
- Shoulder-in

The movements of the gaits are the natural ability, as well as the learned technical execution, of lengthening, shortening, and collection. Movements of this type are:

- Lengthening of the stride in the walk, trot, and canter
- The free walk
- Medium walk, trot, and canter
- Serpentines
- 20-, 15- and 10-meter circles
- Diagonals in trot
- Leg-yielding
- Riding straight on the long sides

It is in these movements that the ability of the horse to show his gaits, regularity, and the scope of his strides can become a significant asset to the ultimate score.

Most tests are deliberately divided almost evenly between the gaits and the technical movements. The difficulties are increased in the way these movements are combined, requiring more and more sophisticated transitions from one to the next.

This is very fair to all competitors, since magnificent gaits alone cannot win a test. Very often, a horse with average gaits that is well trained and ridden by a skilled rider will win over a horse with magnificent gaits or a horse not yet sufficiently developed for the technical requirements of the test or ridden by an unskilled rider. As a matter of fact, a magnificently moving horse often has more difficulties with the technicalities, precision, and coordinated movements than a less gifted one. Often the superb gaits of a horse are ruined by an unskilled rider trying to achieve technical correctness.

On the other hand, when superb gaits, a skilled rider, and technical accomplishment are combined, one sees what dressage is really all about. A combination of this type is almost unbeatable in competition. Unfortunately, it is very rare indeed.

Looking at First Level 1, how would this break down? The technical movements are:

- The centerline and halts at X and G
- Two 10-meter half-circles
- A turn at C and turns from E and X
- The canter departs
- The canter on the diagonal with 2 transitions

The movements for gaits are:

- A serpentine
- Two lengthenings in the trot
- A free walk and medium walk
- A large canter circle of 15 meters and the long side

Since each individual knows his horse best, it should be very easy to see in advance where your points will come from, where the emphasis needs to be placed, and where caution must be exercised to avoid getting into trouble.

This knowledge will become very important in the strategy of riding, which varies enormously from one horse to the next.

MOVEMENTS WITH COEFFICIENTS

Every test has movements with coefficients, and you should know where these are. Try to select a test where the coefficients coincide with the strong points of your horse. If this is not possible, try to avoid any disasters by riding conservatively, correctly and, above all, be certain that the transitions into and out of the movements are perfect.

Remember, all levels, including Training Level, have coefficients of 2 for some or all of the collective marks. This puts inordinate emphasis on the scores in the lower levels because of fewer movements than in comparison with the FEI levels.

Coefficients are assigned to movements for two reasons: the movement is new; or the movement is very important. Let's look at the First Level Tests 1 and 2:

The coefficients here are for the free walk, an important basic gait, and include the transition back to the working gait. This is a perfect test to determine if the horse has really accepted the bit or is just being pulled in by the rider. Any resistance—getting above the bit, jogging, changing rhythm, and length of stride—are a dead giveaway that the basic criteria of a First Level test have not been achieved. The coefficient will reward the good and punish the bad.

In First Level 1, the serpentine of three loops in working trot sitting, and the giving and taking of the reins are both with a coefficient of 2.

Similarly, the lengthening of the stride in the trot is twice associated with a coefficient in First Level 2. The intent here is that the lengthening must have been learned correctly by this point, so you can develop a medium trot as will be required in Second Level. This also helps ensure that the horse that fails to lengthen correctly doesn't have much of a chance to win; a horse will either be penalized four times, or rewarded equally well if he lengthens correctly.

In First Level Test 3, leg-yielding has a coefficient of 2. The coefficient previously given for lengthening in the trot is now

applied to the lengthening in the canter. And another coefficient is again given for the giving and taking of the reins, as in First Level 1. The problem is the rider's inability to realize that poor performance—riding movements with coefficients incorrectly—costs dearly, all the way up to the FEI levels. Since the same coefficient shows up again and again, it is essential that one learns how to ride them correctly at First Level.

The answer to this is to learn your lessons well when they come up the first time, get your rewards for having done well, and come home with scores over 60 percent from each show.

CHAPTER EIGHT:

SELECTING A TEST

FROM the previous chapters, you should now have a clear understanding of what a dressage test really is, and it should be relatively easy to make a correct assessment of how your horse measures up. So, don't go to the tooth fairy or a gypsy to find out which test to ride. You can decide easily at home without trying everything out in the schooling ring.

The selection of a test depends in large part on the competitor's make-up. Some prefer to ride an FEI horse in First or Second Level, equal to their own limitations. Others will take a Second or Third Level horse and put him immediately in the Prix St. George. Both practices are wrong, but each competitor has to make his own decisions.

For practical reasons, and based on the horse's and rider's ability, a good approach is to try and enter the first class at a show at a level in which horse and rider are absolutely secure and capable of performing with no difficulties. This accomplishes two objectives:

First, the chance to be in the ribbons and have a good score. And second, the chance to build the horse's and rider's confidence and not upset the horse unnecessarily in a new environment at the beginning of a show.

There is also no need to ride anything fancy or difficult in the warm-up. One should not school the horse but instead settle him down, relax him, and have him ready to go forward when the bell rings.

Your second entry for a show should be at the level you are working on at home, in order to get a fair appraisal of your work and some helpful suggestions on the score sheet. Your objective should be to make progress and to compare your standing to the other horses competing at the same level.

In a one-day show, you should not enter more than two or a maximum of three classes for one horse, even in the lower levels. In a two-day show, in the lower levels, two classes the first day and two classes the second day is enough for both horse and rider. At the FEI levels, you should never enter a horse in more than two classes on the same day and for a two-day show, three FEI rides is the maximum you should ask for.

The only AHSA rule governing the selection of a test is that you cannot ride in more than two consecutive levels. However, there is no rule that you can only ride Training Level 3 after having shown in Training Level 1 and 2, or that you must ride Second Level 4 before you can show Third Level 1. While the tests are constructed in a progressively more demanding manner, they in no way fit the training progress of every horse.

As long as you stay within the definitions of the AHSA rule, you have eight tests to choose from. Two of these should be appropriate for each horse and rider's skills at any stage.

TESTS TO THE RIGHT AND TESTS TO THE LEFT

In the lower levels, and especially at Training Level, the natural tendency of the horse to go better on one side than on the other is the decisive factor in selecting the test. At this stage of training, most horses are not yet symmetrically supple, evenly bent, or balanced on both sides, much less able to travel on a straight line. They are stiff to one side, naturally bent to the other, will canter nicely to the left but throw their heads up in the canter depart to the right, or vice versa. It is almost like riding two different horses to the left or to the right, and you can be sure judges see this right away.

Your remedy for this is to select a test where the first five or six movements and turns are to the horse's easy side. Plan the half-circle entering the ring to the good side; the first turn at C to the good side; the first circle to the good side, the first corner to the good side; the first canter depart to the good side; the first canter circle to the good side; and the first down transition from the canter to the trot to the good side. Then go on to the movements on the difficult side, which will be fewer and easier.

Imagine the opposite, if the test you selected begins to your horse's weaker side. You may have entered on an already improperly bent horse. The turn at C is stiff and off-balance. There is no

bending on the circle and a definite loss of rhythm and and regularity. Your canter depart is on a horse above the bit, bent to the outside and so on.

If you begin this way, you cannot expect the judge to have a good impression of your movements, your horse's gaits, submission, suppleness, or of your riding ability. Furthermore, you will be upset and struggling against predictable odds and your horse will become more and more tense as the test goes on.

Someone else's horse, who is naturally bent to the other side than yours, will have an apparently easy, smooth ride and walk away with a blue ribbon without being a better rider or having a better trained horse for that matter. So don't put yourself at a disadvantage before you even start.

Later on, in the First and Second levels, the above statements are no longer as relevant, since the horse is expected to be equally supple on both sides.

It's worth mentioning here that you should also take into account your own crookedness. Unevenness in humans such as a slight scoliosis, with a tilted pelvis and different position and length of one leg is very common. Even if minimal, this tips the rider to one side and favors a collapsed hip to the other. A simple

way to reduce the effect of this anatomical unevenness is to shorten the stirrup by one hole on the short side. No where in the *Rule Book* does it say that you have to ride with even stirrups if one of your legs is slightly shorter or your pelvis tilted.

When selecting your test, keep in mind that all tests are built symmetrically, and that judges have very good memories of what they have seen. For example, the angle, bend and fluidity of a shoulder-in must be equal on both sides. Otherwise, it is evident instantly that the horse has not yet achieved equal suppleness to both sides. Points will be lost in the scoring of the movement and in the collective marks. If the difference is extreme, the final score will reflect it. And, a reflection on the ability of rider will show up in the collective marks, particularly on the effectiveness of the rider's aids. The limitations of the weaker side should determine how far you can push on the better side.

You must also be able to differentiate between the collected, medium, and extended gaits, which means the longitudinal suppleness of your horse. If the gait just stays the same throughout the test, or is barely different, at least one or two points will be lost. But if a medium trot or medium canter is called for in the test (like in Second Level), you can go all out and gain points. You should try to go for the maximum points possible in the movement, but be sure that rhythm, regularity, and self-carriage are maintained, and being careful not to push the horse beyond his ability to handle the movement.

THE HORSE'S POINT OF VIEW

Horses are not machines. They know their own physical abilities and shortcomings as well, if not better, than humans do. They will also let certain individuals know exactly how much of a handicap they are on their back and in their mouths. Let your horse decide which test he likes and which is a miserable pile of accumulated harassment.

Every horse has movements that he loves to do and others that just make him grunt when asked to perform them. So look at the

test from your horse's point of view. Since there are eight tests to choose from, there should be at least two or three you can select with many movements your horse is capable of performing to the best of his ability, and that include the fewest number of the movements he honestly dislikes. Why pick a test where the horse hates every step of the way, and shows this, like it or not? Remember, unless you are on speaking terms with your horse, you have not even started dressage yet!

So, carefully selecting the test that shows you and your horse at your combined best is the first step to successful competitive riding.

CHAPTER NINE

LEARNING THE TEST

I T is absolutely essential that you devote the necessary time to learning a test. Riders who rely on readers and ride from letter to letter seldom finish in the ribbons. Furthermore, once you understand how a test is built, it will be much easier for you to analyze, and select the one best suited for your horse and the level of training. You can then devise a winning strategy of how to present it.

There are many ways to learn a test, but I have found the following way to work the best for me. Start by putting 16 to 20 rectangles in the proportions of a dressage arena on a sheet of paper, letters and all, and xerox a dozen or so copies. Then, decide on different colors for the walk, the trot, and the canter, and invent your own symbols for halt, rein back, counter-canter, or whatever is required in the test. Draw in each movement, in the color chosen for that gait, in one rectangle. Be careful to show exactly where each movement ends (check the test sheet), so that you will know exactly where the scoring starts for the next movement. For example, notice that the first centerline score ends at C, after halting at X and proceeding in the required gait, almost the point where the horse begins turning at G. As a result, the turn at the end of the centerline is the first part of the next move-

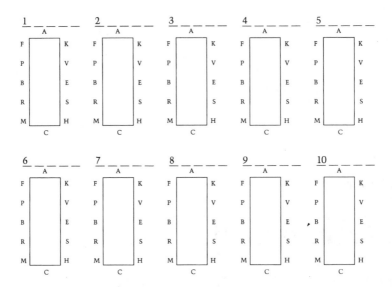

ment. This is important to know, since a poor turn will ruin that second movement, be it a circle, shoulder-in, or a medium trot on the diagonal. Other scores are given only for a single transition at a given letter and so on. By looking at your finished sheet, you can see all the movements and how they flow from one to the next, with the transitions, and how they will be scored.

Just knowing the pattern to ride is not good enough to put you in the ribbons at most major competitions. But once you understand the basic composition of the ride, you will have a solid basis on which to build a strategic plan.

Once you have analyzed and understand the test, it is easy not only to memorize the pattern but also to be completely clear on the objectives and difficulties. When this is properly done and the test learned, the tests become quite logical in their layout, coefficients, and directive ideas.

Once the test is started correctly, it is almost impossible to make a mistake if the basic concepts of the test construction have been learned. So, take your sheet of the movements with you; it will fit easily in your coat pocket. Then you can glance at it for reassurance when going from the warm-up area to the ring. The written tests are much too time consuming to look at, especially if needed glasses are not with you!

If you do go off course, don't panic. It's only 2 points out of a possible 100 or more, and you still have a chance to reorganize. There is no time limit on you so there is no need to rush. Take another minute or so to show the judge and your friends how good you really are.

So far, we have figured out the pattern of riding, but not the test itself. There is much more to it, and you must work with an original AHSA test sheet in hand. The various booklets or xeroxed copies of one side of the test sheet will not help you in this next step.

Let's take Training Level Test 4 as our example; look at the outside cover of the test. Under the heading of Purpose, you find the basic description of how to ride the test, how your horse is

AMERICAN HORSE SHOWS ASSOCIATION
220 East 42nd Street
New York, NY 10017-5876

1995
TRAINING LEVEL TEST 4

AMERICAN
HORSE
SHOWS
ASSOCIATION, INC.

Purpose: To confirm that the horse's muscles are supple and loose, and that it moves freely forward in a clear and steady rhythm, accepting contact with the bit. (Drawing shows movement #3)

Conditions:
Arena: Standard or small
Average time: 5:30

Maximum Possible Points: 250

Name of Competition

Date of Competition

Number and Name of Horse

Name of Rider

FINAL SCORE

Points   Percent

Name of Judge

Signature of Judge

©1994 BY THE AMERICAN HORSE SHOWS ASSOCIATION, INC. ALL RIGHTS RESERVED.
REPRODUCTION WITHOUT PERMISSION PROHIBITED BY LAW.

expected to go, and how you will be judged. This is the fundamental concept of the level and test. It tells us very clearly that
the horse's muscles should be supple and loose, moving freely
forward in a clear and steady rhythm. He should accept contact
with the bit. The test says nothing about him being collected or
showing engagement or impulsion. So don't worry about things
not expected or required from the competitor at this stage.

Also note that the front of the test sheet indicates whether or
not the ride can be in a standard or a smaller arena. All Training
Level tests and First Level Tests 1 and 2, can be ridden in the
smaller arenas, so be prepared! It is nasty surprise to prepare for
an arena of 20 by 60 meters, only to wind up in a 20 by 40 meter
arena, where everything happens much faster.

For example, a 20-meter circle at A or C will now extend up to
X. The circle from E or B comes within four meters of G. Draw a
diagram of the movements in simulated rectangles of 20 by 60
meters and 20 by 40 meters, then ride each size. This will help
instill the feeling of the size difference between the two. If you
are aware of where to go in the event of a change in arena size,
feel free to smile at the competitors who seem bewildered and
lost and must improvise the best they can on the spot! Being
unprepared like that is not the way to win ribbons, and has nothing to do with your riding ability or how well your horse has been
trained. Prepare for an eventuality that will happen without fail,
sooner or later, if you compete in the lower levels. Again, it is
your responsibility, not your horse's!

The front cover of Training Level Test 4 even shows exactly
movement 3, a loop from F to X to M, should be ridden. What
could be clearer?

Open the test sheet for Training Level Test 4 and see that the
Purpose of the test is restated from the front cover (must be
important!).

Below that, in small print, is called Instructions and it reads:
"Transitions in and out of the halt may be made through the
walk." So the option of sliding to the halt through the walk
exists, thank heaven.

Once you reach First Level, that statement will never appear again, so take full advantage of it now if it helps in making the halt straight, balanced, and square. The easy days when you can do this will soon be over once you move up.

The most important part is found under Directive Ideas, the comments that refer to each movement and score. Here you will find what is important and what exactly the judges are looking for. By the time you finish reading these for each movement, two facts—quality of gait and transitions—will probably stick in your mind.

These are very important reminders, since besides telling you what is important, these directive ideas invariably point to possible trouble spots, such as in the canter of movements 13 and 14 in Training Level Test 4:
Besides a good canter and a relatively round circle, the key to this movement will be the transition from the canter to a sitting trot at B.

DIRECTIVE IDEAS:

B Circle right 20m	Quality of canter, roundness of circle
B Working trot sitting and proceed straight	Balance during transition, quality of trot.

A final word on collective marks: they summarize the test just ridden. If your scores are in the 5 to 7 range, the collective marks will be approximately the same, giving you a good idea of your horse's strong points and where he needs improvement. The test sheet provides a good indicator of what needs to be worked on when you get home. Look closely at the judge' s comments, the scores, and directive ideas. These are your best indicators of what is good and not so good in your performance. Also, the fact that the collective marks have coefficients of 2 makes the basics weigh very heavily on your total score, either good or bad.

1995 FIRST LEVEL TEST 1

Purpose: To confirm that the horse, in addition to the requirements of Training Level, has developed thrust (pushing power) and achieved a degree of balance and throughness.(Diagram shows movement #5)

NO.

Conditions:
Arena: Standard or small
Average Time: 5:30
Maximum Possible Points: 280

		TEST	DIRECTIVE IDEAS	POINTS	COEFFICIENT	TOTAL	REMARKS
1.	A X	Enter working trot Halt, Salute Proceed working trot	Straightness on centerline, transitions, quality of halt and trot				
2.	C E	Track left Half circle left 10m returning to the track at H	Quality of turn at C, quality of trot, execution and size of figure				
3.	B	Half circle right 10m returning to the track at M	Quality of trot, execution and size of figure				
4.	HXF F	Lengthen stride in trot rising Working trot sitting	Straightness, quality of trots and transitions				
5.	A-C	Serpentine of 3 equal loops width of arena	Quality of trot, execution of figure		2		
6.	C	Medium walk	Transition, quality of walk				
7.	MXF F	Free walk Medium walk	Straightness, quality of transitions		2		
8.	A	Working trot	Quality of transition and trot				
9.	K	Working canter right lead	Calmness and smoothness of depart				
10.	E	Circle right 15m	Quality of canter, roundness and size of circle				
11.	MXK X	Change rein Working trot	Straightness, balance during transition				
12.	F	Working canter left lead	Calmness and smoothness of depart				
13.	B	Circle left 15m	Quality of canter, roundness and size of circle				
14.	HXF X	Change rein Working trot	Straightness, balance during transition				
15.	A before A A	Circle right 20m working trot rising, letting the horse gradually take the reins out of the hands Take up the reins proceed ahead	Gradually giving and later taking the reins, horse stretching forward and downward with light contact, while maintaining balance, rhythm and quality of trot		2		
16.	KXM M	Lengthen stride in trot rising Working trot sitting	Straightness, quality of trots and transitions				
17.	E X G	Turn left Turn left Halt, Salute	Quality of trot, quality of turns at E and X, straightness on centerline, transition, quality of halt				

Leave arena at walk at A

COLLECTIVE MARKS:

Gaits (freedom and regularity)		2	
Impulsion (desire to move forward, elasticity of the steps, relaxation of the back)		2	
Submission (attention and confidence; harmony, lightness and ease of movements; acceptance of the bit)		2	
Rider's position and seat; correctness and effect of the aids		2	

FURTHER REMARKS:

SUBTOTAL   _____

ERRORS   (-_____)

TOTAL POINTS _____

PART FOUR: THE COMPETITION

CHAPTER TEN:

STRATEGY IN RIDING A TEST

NOW that you have picked a test, you will need to make a specific plan on how to ride it. Just going from letter to letter makes no sense. It's your understanding of the inherent problems and opportunities that gives you an edge over your co-competitors who have not done their homework.

THE ANGLE OF VISION

Why is it that one person watching a dressage test will never come to the same decision about the scoring as the next person? The spectators on the long side of the ring think it was a poor ride but the judge at C gives a high score of 70 percent. Friends taking a video from the corner consider the performance the ride of the show, but the judge sitting at C is totally unimpressed. The judge at E gives the same rider a 4 for the entry, while the one at C gives him an 8. No wonder the favorite pastime at the end of a show is to lament over incompetent judges and their inability to grasp the incomparable qualities of your horse. Woe be unto the competitors having to perform in front of unappreciative audiences and judges!

The smart riders just smile and keep winning by taking full advantage of underlying factors: their circles are oval, but they don't cross the centerline; their entries are absolutely straight on centerline, but the halt is neither square nor at X; their diagonals away from the judge finish a few meters from the letter; their half halts are very demanding when their backs are to the judges, but very soft when going in the opposite direction; their haunches-in towards the judge are exaggerated in angle, but those going away from the judge are less than 35 degrees. It takes an experienced judge, possibly riding competitively himself, to see these things for what they are. He must realize that there are limits to what he can do from C, since he must judge from what is visible, and he must not be influenced by what he thinks is going on.

UNDERSTANDING THE ANGLE OF VISION FROM C

Dressage tests are movements in a space designed, oriented, and executed in the lower levels toward one observation point: C. What one sees from C has nothing to do with what one sees from the sideline, or from an awkward angle from around the arena. Better shows offer at least two judges per ring down to Training Level, and three to five judges for the upper levels and international competition. Judges' scores are usually very close if a rider performs true to a test, but can differ significantly if the ride has been choreographed only for the judge at C.

Looking at the diagram of the ring, it is clear that the angle of vision can work to your advantage if you know how to use it. Likewise, it can drag you under if you don't know what it can do to your ride.

Take your test and look at it from the viewpoint of C. Draw in the movements toward or away from the judge as the case may be. You will instantly see where you must be accurate. You will see where the blind spots are that will allow for adjustments to be made, where you may need to exaggerate, and where you can under-perform and give your horse a break.

As an example, let's consider the centerline and halt at X. The judge sits exactly at the end of the line from A to C. At that position, there is no depth perception as to exactly where the ring starts, or where X is in the centerline. And, the lower the judge is seated, the more impossible it is for him to determine. Furthermore, even if a horse halts absolutely straight on the centerline, it is impossible to tell if the hind legs are really square. The hind legs are hidden behind the front legs, so they could be engaged, or they could be out behind the horse. The primary concern, then, is to be dead on the centerline and dead straight in the halt. The fact that the horse is not square or at X is irrelevant when analyzing the angle of vision from C. This, of course, would be different in the event of two or more judges.

Now let's look at the travers from B to F as it was in the old test, and then from B to M as it is today in Second Level 4. In the first instance, the judge only saw your back and the rear end of the horse, not a very inspiring view. The judge was unable to see if the horse was bent, on the bit, if half halts were given, if there were irregularities in the front, resistance, or unsteady hands of the competitor. So, you could take

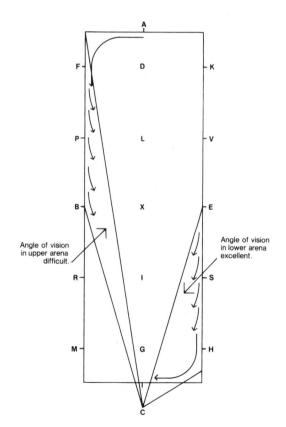

Angle of vision in upper arena difficult.

Angle of vision in lower arena excellent.

it easy on your horse if he was not really on the bit and just let it go. If some of the bend or position was lost, remember, it wasn't really visible. The only corrections really necessary had to do with the angle and regularity of the rhythm, the two factors clearly visible from C.

But, look at the same movement ridden from B to M as in the current tests. The judge sees everything: angle, bend, regularity in front, steadiness on the bit, acceptance and correctness of the aids, every movement of your little finger and the reins, the position of your hips and shoulders in relation to the movements of the horse, the transitions at B and M, and the quality of gait.

This could be a real disaster, with no way to bluff your way through it and magically get an undeserved 7. This is why, in the current Second Level Test, all the travers and shoulder-in's are performed toward the judge, with difficult transitions and no chance to hide.

RIDING FOR TWO JUDGES

With two judges, it is customary to have the chief judge at C responsible for running the ring, calling errors and making all decisions. The judge at E or B scores with no administrative responsibility. With three judges, the distribution is the chief judge at C, one at E or B, and the third in the corner facing down the long side at H or M, opposite to the judge at E or B. With the five judges mandatory for international competitions, World Championships, Olympics and other important shows, the judges are located at C, H, M, E and B.

While FEI and upper level riders with experience are used to riding in a fish bowl, being seen from all angles, beginners and lower level competitors hardly realize what that can do to their scores. Now, precision and accuracy become very important, even in the lower levels.

Instinctively, most of us aim at a performance to look good from C and, consciously or unconsciously, we have learned what we can get away with when seen from this angle of vision only.

However, in competitive riding with two judges, this will not work anymore. We must become conscious that we ride in a two dimensional setting. For instance, riding the halt exactly at X, not before and not afterwards, perfectly square with the horse absolutely on the bit, is just as important as riding straight on the centerline. I have seen riders extremely conscious of the view from C but totally oblivious to impressions created for the judges at Eor B. They use many techniques to help their horse that are not visible from C, but end up being scored down because it is incorrect as seen from the other position. The difference between the two judges' scores in such a ride may suddenly become enormous, even if they are mostly quite close together for the riders in the rest of the class. A typical example would be, for instance, riding a 10-meter circle while you are terribly conscious not to exceed the centerline, you don't hesitate to make it an oval or a 14-meter diameter on the longitudinal axis. Obviously, no judge sitting at E or B will let you get away with this. While from C such a movement might look acceptable, if not perfect, from B you will get caught instantly.

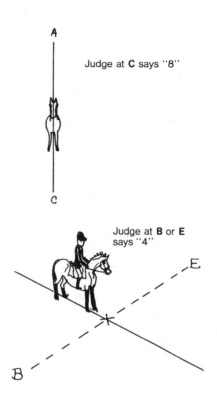

Judge at **C** says "8"

Judge at **B** or **E** says "4"

Personally, I believe that having two judges or more is eminently fair to the competitors and those who are correctly riding a round circle. A correct test will always come out on top. On the other hand, some riders who had previously received 6's, 7's and 8's for their performance of certain movements, will be quite

upset if suddenly they are rated insufficient. But, if you are smart and study the comments on the test afterward, it will be the last time that you make such a mistake, or try to avoid the difficulty of the movement.

What happens is that large discrepancies between judges are always an indication that there is a fundamental flaw in the execution of your movements.

To analyze what it means to ride in front of two judges, make yourself a diagram of the movement and study the angle of vision from B as well as from C. You will see immediately that you basically have no escape but to ride correctly.

Damage Control

Perhaps the best advice on strategy is, simply put, be careful, limit the damage, and be very aware that things may not go as planned. Above all, concentrate on not upsetting your horse, throwing him off balance, or getting rattled if you make a mistake.

The basic strategy for damage control is to not carry the problem from one movement to the next. By now, you know where the score begins and where it finishes. If everything goes wrong, you can even come to a halt on the track (but don't circle back which would be an error, of course). Start again in a quiet, balanced and controlled manner instead of going on and on while becoming progressively more disorganized. It is by far better to get a 1, 2, or 3 on one movement and go back to 6's and 7's for the rest of the test than to make a series of 4's.

A typical example is an incorrect canter depart in Training Level. Go right back to the walk, if necessary, then a few trot steps, then canter on correctly. A good rider can do this easily between K and A.

Here is where the key in planning comes in. Decide to canter on at K or a stride before. The angle of vision will allow for this, and it certainly will not be marked down in Training Level. You have the time to make a correction before A, and do not have to start the next movement on the wrong foot.

In contrast, if you begin the canter after the turn just before A and fail, all of your correction will be done in the next movement. At best you will get a 3 in one movement and a 4 in the next, instead of 3 or 4 in the first transition, and a 6 or better for the canter work in the circle in the next movement.

Correct, effective, and smooth handling of such mishaps reflects favorably on the competitor, whereas dragging a messed-up situation on and on gets very short shrift from the judge in the collective marks as well as for the movement itself.

Knowing where troubles may occur, you can develop a strategy of how to minimize them before hand. When difficulties do happen in the ring, the response to correct them should be instantaneous. Once in the ring, it is simply too late to start thinking about what to do to correct mistakes.

MAKING THE BEST OF GOING OFF COURSE

I mentioned sometime ago to a physician friend in a joking way, that it is absolutely predictable who will ride off course simply by watching the entry. Anyone who stops breathing at A develops a cerebral anoxemia and, sooner or later, some loss of concentration and memory. By all means, keep breathing while riding and stay relaxed.

Seriously, going off course is no disaster. It only costs you 2 penalty points out of approximately 200 points. Furthermore, it can give you a chance to breath, rearrange, and give your horse a chance to catch his balance. It also enables you to start all over, hopefully better than the last time.

The worst enemy you have is yourself if you get rattled and rush to do the test over correctly. In most instances, you are not gaining anything by going about it this way. Ride to the judge who will tell you where to start again, and if needed, the correct sequence of movements to follow. You might be surprised at how helpful a judge can be. Most judges have been, or still are, competitive riders and they have all gone off course, too. You are just joining an illustrious society.

THE NEXT MOVEMENT

From a riding point of view, movements do not start at the letters as stated in the AHSA test; they really start at least a half movement or more earlier.

Therefore, when looking at your test, decide when your preparation starts for the next movement. It is the key to a correct transition and to the next score. Your ability to accomplish this depends largely on the state of training of the horse, your riding ability, and your proficiency in the half halts.

Competitive dressage riding involves thinking ahead, not just riding from letter to letter, and the preparation is best done at home, not at the show. This does not mean that one should not try it out once a plan has been made–by all means do–though you may have to modify it a little bit. But just doing the same pattern over and over again will not increase your test score, unless thinking and strategies have been added in.

Big Movers Versus Short Gaited but Technically Correct Horses

With so many European Warmbloods imported for dressage and often possessing tremendous gaits, many competitors feel at a disadvantage on their American Thoroughbreds or half-bred Quarter Horses or Appaloosas.

I do not agree with this "disadvantage point," because I have competed successfully on a Quarter Horse, a Thoroughbred Trakhener-cross, and a Hanoverian. Each has his advantages and disadvantages. You make the best of what you have. Seldom Seen, a small Connemara, was quite possibly the horse with the best technical skills at Grand Prix in the United States. He had a good trot and only an average canter. But he beat all the big movers up to his retirement on his precision and correctness, not on his gaits.

In addition, the bigger the horse and more forward the stride, the smaller the dressage ring becomes. A 10-meter circle is nothing for a 15.2 hand Quarter Horse. But try to ride a 17.2 hand 1500-pound Dutch Warmblood with gaits a mile long on a 10-meter circle—he almost has to step on his tail to make it around the circle!

Most of the Warmbloods are too big for the skills, size, and weight of their riders, and here you can have another advantage. So, do not try to beat the big boys on their own turf. Instead, be better where they have problems, namely, in the technical movements and precision.

For instance, look at the collected walk. The big horses pace very easily when the reins are picked up. How many Quarter Horses or Thoroughbreds pace? Very few.

Deep corners, 10- and 8-meter circles can be ridden easily by a Quarter Horse with basic training and suppleness. But try this on a 17 hand Warmblood and you will be surprised. Later on, in the flying change on the diagonal, or a zig-zag down the centerline, there is hardly enough space for the big horses, and they often finish after the letters or almost in the judge' s lap. Again, this is no real problem for smaller horses with less scope.

So, don't despair, but plan differently for each type of horse. Let's take a practical example, such as the trot movements in First Level 1, and look at two imaginary horses. Horse A is a 17 hand import, big, solid, and rhythmic, with an enormous ability to extend. The other, Horse B, is a Thoroughbred/Quarter Horse cross, 15.3 hands, very flexible, easy to engage, in proportion to the size of the rider, but with limited gaits.

The first part of the test consists of three 10-meter half-circles and four corners, a test to determine if there is equal flexibility on both sides, a proper bending while staying on the aids, and a maintaining of rhythm and impulsion. These movements are interspersed with short, straight sections, followed by a lengthening of stride to establish forwardness, and finishing in a serpentine of three loops.

HORSE A

This horse will probably have difficulty in the 10-meter half-circles, and corners leading to a loss of impulsion and drifting outward on the bad side.

STRATEGY:

Make a very controlled forward transition after the halt at X, taking extra care to be rhythmic and slow. This is no time to show off your gaits. Rather, you should avoid any mistakes such as the haunches drifting out, crossing the centerline, or losing the regularity of rhythm, self-carriage, and impulsion. The basic concept is to stay out of trouble in the first two movements after the centerline.

HORSE B

This horse has no difficulty ahead. The corner and 10-meter half-circles are no sweat for him, and it is easy to balance this horse from one bend to the other. He maintains self-carriage by himself, and you can improve him on the half-circles and corners by demanding more engagement of the inside hind leg, leading into the lengthening.

STRATEGY:

Start off light, forward, and energetic after the halt at X, and exaggerate the bending ability of your horse. You can show off and relax. Be sure to keep the rhythm, since your horse does not have a metronome in his belly like the Warmblood. After the second movement collect your horse more on the short side to show a better difference to following lengthening.

Now take the next two movements, the lengthening of stride and the serpentine. The 20-meter half-circles of the serpentine are enormously easier than what was performed in the previous movement. By now you should know what a correct serpentine looks like and how to ride it.

HORSE A

As the movements in this section of the test are easier for this horse, you can ride him more forward in the same rhythm. Be certain that you show an equal bending to both sides since this may have been a problem earlier. Now use his gaits to show off and have this big machine power himself through the lengthening of stride and the serpentine.

STRATEGY:

> In the last turn at **M** and the short side, try to put the
> horse together with half halts and your seat. If you are suc-
> cessful, this will make the transition to the lengthening at
> **H** so much more dramatic. If you miss, concentrate on the
> rhythm and you will still be doing fine.

Next, move your horse onto the diagonal, and he will give you
a lengthening with impulsion as soon as be is allowed to do so.
But how much do you want? Remember, transitions count as
much as the quality of gait. Ask yourself if you can handle the
second transition at F after going full out in the lengthening.

What good would it do to have a superb lengthening with no
transition back, plowing through the corner at full speed with
your horse on the forehand and being pulled behind the vertical
by a desperate rider?

A better strategy is to aim for one or two strides before F and
sacrifice precision for more room in the down transition. Position
your horse to the inside, which will lead to a clean corner and a
balanced halt.

The better and more extravagant gaits you have, the more
problems you will face at F. You should always temper your
enthusiasm for dramatic gaits with wisdom that technical difficulties are ahead.

HORSE B

Technically, there is no problem for this horse in the serpentine
but by all means keep the same rhythm and stride; don't go more
forward like your big friend. Bank on your steadiness, rhythm,
suppleness, and self-carriage, not on impressive gaits. The real
problem you are faced with is the lengthening of the stride on the
diagonal.

STRATEGY:

You know your lengthening is not as dramatic as Horse A's, so shorten the stride and get your horse rounder before you reach C and through the corner at H. Start with half halts in the turn at H, followed by a shoulder-fore position on the short side, and half halt in the last turn.

Moving onto the diagonal, concentrate on the rhythm first, and make a very gradual transition forward. Never let the horse rush or run. Take whatever lengthening the horse can give, as long as the quality of gait is there. Do not push the horse beyond his capability and balance, or he may fall apart. Don't worry about the transition at F; your horse will be only too happy to come back, as long as he is not interfered with.

You can apply this kind of analysis and strategic development to any test and any horse. Once your plan has been established, don't let it be hampered by the good advice from friends and co-competitors.

Try out your plan and go for it. There are only two possibilities: either it works, or it doesn't work. In the latter case, analyze the test based on the judge' s scores and remarks about what went wrong and why. Modify the test as needed in the movements that need work and try again.

Very soon, your test will be impeccable and your performance will be on par with the pros.

Suddenly, dressage riding will be fun. It can be relaxing and you can actually breath while riding. And the judges aren't as dumb anymore as they used to be, just a short while ago!

CHAPTER 11:

COMPETITION FACILITIES AND WARM-UP

INSPECTION OF THE ARENA AND RIDING AREA: LOOK BEFORE YOU RIDE

I T is impossible to plan an intelligent ride without knowing the problems and difficulties inherent in the facilities available at a given show. They are usually totally different from those at home and, in most cases, the warm-up and competition rings have different footing.

Therefore, once your horse has been settled in, it is mandatory that you inspect on foot the riding set-up.

The Warm-Up Area

Footing: Besides location, size and distance from the competition ring, the most important feature of the warm-up area is the footing. While not important by itself for the warm-up, it has a profound effect on the performance of the horse in the ring. The greater the difference with the show ring, the more difficult it will be to ride the test well.

Sand: Warming up on sand is a luxury very few shows offer, even for the FEI classes. When it exists, compare the consistency and deepness with the footing in the show ring. Any change from hard to deep footing or the reverse between the warm-up area and the show ring will shorten your horse's gaits and reduce his desire to move forward.

Artificial Footing: If you will be warming up on an artificial surface like treated wood chips, check the looseness of the footing. If slippery, ride turns and circles more carefully to avoid any loss of balance and your horse's confidence in the footing on which he has to perform.

Turf: Most warm-up areas are turf and vary from a rolling cow pasture with woodchuck holes to a manicured polo field. Often the warm-up area is closely related to the competition ring–but is always worse. If you can warm-up on a polo field, the rings are usually just as good or better. If the warm-up is in a field or a pasture, you must anticipate problems with the show ring too.

If the warm-up area is not flat but has bumps and dips, you should ride them from every direction and in all gaits to get your horse used to it and to improve his balance. You'll also need to reinforce your technique for supporting your horse when heading for difficult going. If there is similar going in the ring, your horse will be well prepared and lose neither rhythm or balance in negotiating the various bumps and bad corners. Be assured the judge will notice immediately those horses in good balance and rhythm, and who can maneuver over the difficult areas in the competition ring.

The Dressage Arena

With the impression of the warm-up area still fresh in your mind, you should examine the dressage arena immediately. This consists of two separate parts: one, the area around the ring, and two, the ring itself. While looking at it on foot, you can run through a mental checklist. Look at the arena from all sides and be more circumspect with possible problems the younger or less experienced your horse is.

Plan to spend the maximum mount of time before your test riding outside the arena. The 90 seconds permitted is a very long time; you can ride once around the ring and still have 30 seconds left. Never turn around and rush through A once the bell rings.

Finish what you are doing. Relax and leisurely prepare your entry as planned. You have plenty of time for everything.

For any change in footing from soft to hard, hard to deep, or turf to sand, expect your horse to automatically shorten up, resist moving forward, and even hesitate. You'll need to ride forward medium or extended gaits as the last movements before entering the ring to give your horse confidence in the new footing. This also makes sense when you consider that the second score in many tests is for an extended or medium trot.

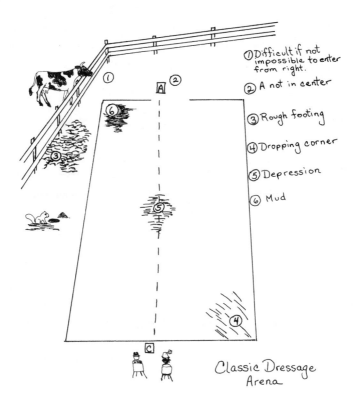

① Difficult if not impossible to enter from right.

② A not in center

③ Rough footing

④ Dropping corner

⑤ Depression

⑥ Mud

Classic Dressage Arena

Grass arenas are a special case; they are never even. Look for where the rough spots are and particularly the undulations, since you have to ride over them.

The Surroundings

Check to see if there is anything unusual in the area: a house with laundry in the wind, a hedge with cows behind that you can hear and smell but not see, unusual cross-country jumps, a hidden highway with rumbling trucks or motor bikes, and, more common, flowers placed at each letter. All these things must be shown to your horse on foot if at all possible. If the surroundings are very different from home, take your horse and lead him around the show area, letting him look leisurely at everything. George Wahl, the well known trainer of Christine Stuckelberger, many times World and European Champion, took the famous horse Granat for hours and hours around the show area, not only once but often many times, before every major competition. Certainly he knew very well what he was doing.

Relaxation

Dressage competitions should be fun, otherwise it makes no sense to participate. While a certain competitive spirit is good, it is not a matter of life and death.

Even though we may agree with the above statement, we all tense up before competitions, and the more so as they become qualifying, finals, or regional championships. Few of us have a motivation psychologist in our tack trunk to be used as needed. But you should develop a technique to stay relaxed.

When you warm-up, ride without stirrups for 5 to 10 minutes in the warm-up and then adjust your stirrups as long as possible for the rest of your warm-up. When you go from the warm-up area to the dressage ring, shorten your stirrups one hole shorter than normal. It feels like a new lease on life and gives you a sense of security.

The reason for doing this is very simple. Everybody feels tense to some degree and this tenseness prevents you from sitting as deep as usual. The heels come up a little as do the knees and your grip. A shorter stirrup compensates and prevents you from reaching for the irons or even losing them. While most professionals or experienced riders don't need this approach, it is appropriate for amateurs and new riders in the dressage field. I have even seen these tenseness problems arise for riders at the Olympics, when tension is at its maximum.

Warming Up

Warming up for competition is totally different from schooling a horse, working on a certain problem, participating in a clinic, or simply going through a daily routine of exercising. Dressage competitions are often won or lost in the final warm-up. The further you move up in the tests, the more difficult it becomes. And the fine tuning of your preparation to peak in the ring is really an art in itself. But at the lower levels, it's much easier if you can follow a simple, consistent system with your horse.

In order to allow for just that, specific times are allocated for each rider and you will never be forced to go early if you want to use all your allotted time. The judge may ask you if you are ready to go, but you are perfectly correct to decline if you feel your horse is not yet at his best, or you have not yet been able to complete your predetermined warm-up schedule. But, after your official time has come, the judge will ring the bell and you have 90 seconds to appear in the ring, with a penalty of elimination if you fail to do so.

If classes or riders are moved up, the show management must announce it at least 1 hour in advance. On the other hand, there may be serious delays due to unexpected circumstances and it is therefore always important to ask the ring or warm-up area steward if your class is running on time or not, to adjust your warm-up plan accordingly, and not to start too early. The most common mistake of all beginners is to warm-up for too long.

Unfortunately, there are practically no clinics or lessons given on the various techniques of warming up and most riders are not quite sure what to do. The following suggestions may be helpful to you in preparing your own schedule and sequence of exercises for your horse and you.

In order to put a sensible warm-up together you must, obviously, know your horse, how fit he is, and the average time it takes for him to move confidently forward and respond properly to your aids. This may be considerably different for a Thoroughbred or a Warmblood, and for older, well-trained horses compared to young and green ones.

The second requirement is to know the definition and objectives of your test and to be very familiar with the problems your horse may face in the various movements and transitions.

Quite often I see lower level riders practicing shoulder-in, haunches-in, lateral movements, and even flying changes in the warm-up area. Then, once they come into the ring, they cannot even ride a straight centerline, or a proper circle, or make even the most fundamental transitions at First Level. It really makes very little sense and you wonder if they even thought about looking at the test they will ride and where their points are coming from.

In general, particularly on Thoroughbreds, don't use too much whip or spur, or be too tight. They are excitable enough and it is more important to develop a soft, steady contact. In contrast, with Warmbloods who are a little bit lazy or a bit more difficult to get moving, additional aids are perfectly all right. The whole warm-up should not take more than thirty minutes or so. That is just enough to get the horse fresh and relaxed.

Be careful not to peak too early. The horse's physical and mental attention span hardly exceeds ten minute per exercise, and you may end up sitting on a dead horse if you overdo it. Don't blame the horse for performing poorly, since it is your fault for not having properly warmed him up or having pushed him way over his peak long before he had to enter the ring.

Warming-up actually starts a few days before you trailer to the show. Since in the lower levels relaxation, regularity of rhythm, balance, harmony of horse and rider, and steadiness on the aids are the key elements of success, it is wrong to school the horse on new and more difficult movements than needed up to the last day. Instead, build up his confidence in the days before the show by lots of praise even if he is not perfect. He will then not be apprehensive and tense when you climb on his back, anticipating severe correction or grinding continuously on one problem or another where he is not yet secure. If such movements are in your test and you cannot ride them, you should not have selected that test in the first place.

It is harmony, freshness, relaxation, and desire to perform something he knows well that your horse should bring to the show. If you have ridden all the sections of the test and all the transitions, and maybe the full test two or three times, neither you nor your horse should have any doubt that you will be working well together, as long as you bring confidence to the show and don't tense up. So start thinking of what to do several days early and concentrate on the easy, repetitive movements which you will have to perform during the competition.

THE PHYSIOLOGY OF THE WARM-UP

What is the difference, physiologically, between a horse that comes out of his stall and one that is perfectly warmed-up and ready to compete?

In the first instance, the horse is, metabolically speaking, in a "vagotonic phase." The digestion is going, most of the blood supply is in the internal organs such as the liver, spleen, gut, mesentaric arteries, and so on. Glucose turnover is low, circulation in the muscles and limbs is reduced with low oxygenation and low carbohydrate metabolism. Adrenalin is low, and total energy output and production is at the bare minimum to support only a comfortable existence. The joints are stiff, ligaments and tendons have been locked to stand up with minimal effort, and the neck muscles are in a semitonic state to support the heavy head.

Obviously, this is no shape in which to go down the centerline!

How do we get where we want to be 30 minutes later, showing a relaxed horse, eager to perform, fresh, moving forward, supple, in self-carriage and on the bit, mastering movements, gaits and transitions like it was nothing, and not being worn out or tired?

For reasons of simplicity, we will subdivide the warming-up into four phases. But, in reality, it is a progressive, continuous process, where much depends on your feel and knowledge of your own horse.

Phase 1. Since the horse is like a huge engine, no change can be brought about abruptly without harm. The first objective is, therefore, to relax and stretch. Extensive grooming is a good start, even a massage, or, if you want, some TEAM application. We have to get the joints, muscles and tendons to move and flex. Consider moving forward on a long rein in the walk. Let your horse balance himself, stretch the back and neck muscles, relax the shoulders and get the muscles and ligaments that suspend the horse between his front legs working properly in coordination, as well as those which activate the back. Don't forget there is no bony connection between the front legs and the body of the horse. And, the suspensory mechanism in front has to carry at least 60 percent of the total weight of horse and rider.

It is in these first five minutes of the warm-up that a significant change takes place. The production instead of storage of energy begins to take place. Higher oxygen demand causes more blood flow and enlargement of the vessels in the muscles, and energy production leads to a warmer temperature of the body. The horse's metabolism is gradually changing from a digestive or resting pattern to one of physical activity. Adrenalin production is gradually picking up. After five minutes or so, begin trotting. Try to keep a steady rhythm and, above all, don't go into a sitting trot. At this stage, we want to make the work of the muscles as easy as possible and avoid having the horse defend himself against the rider by tensing up his back muscles. Interject a few short canter periods, on both leads. Within a short time, you can feel the difference in a progressively more elastic and forward trot. Generally, if you do this for 10 minutes, more or less, you have the horse ready to enter the second phase of the warm-up, which primarily consists of making him begin to respond to your aids.

Phase 2. After a short break in the walk, we begin to ask the horse to develop more engagement and support from the hind legs. Begin first in the walk, on one side and then the other side. This is best done by leg-yielding in the walk on a small circle and, later on, in a shoulder-in and haunches-in, continuing the movement into a renvers. These exercises are very good to soften up the horse, making him supple and balanced. After having done this for a short period in the walk, repeat these movements in the trot. Later on you can use it even in the canter, riding a little bit of shoulder-in in the canter to encourage straightness. Be sure that when you enter the ring, you can really keep the hind quarters under you and avoid going crooked. The first phase in the walk shouldn't take more than five minutes, followed by the same work in the trot. After a short break, we are ready to proceed to phase 3.

Phase 3. Now your horse has been exercised thoroughly but without any great demands for twenty minutes. His metabolism is in shape. He is not tired. You have not punished his back by doing nothing but sitting trot on a straight line and pulling on his mouth. You have ten minutes to get the horse exactly into the stage where he can perform the requirements in the level you are showing. Again, start by putting the horse on the aids in the walk on a small circle, and then riding a working or collected trot in which you insist on self-carriage, acceptance of the bit, and response to the aids. As soon as this is achieved, start riding transitions: transitions from working trot into a lengthening of the trot, into a collected trot, from a trot into a halt, a halt into a trot, from a canter to a trot, from canter to walk, walk to canter, and so on. Just ride transitions, and ride him forward. Change the gaits. Develop his suppleness. First do this on a large circle, so you are always sure to have the inside hind leg under the horse, and then proceed to do the same thing on straight lines. Within a short time, your horse will be very responsive, self-carrying, and perfectly aware of the transitions which are coming.

Then, a short break. In the last two minutes before you proceed to the ring, ride the first five or six movements of your test. They will be fresh in the memory of the horse and you will feel confident about yourself, and that you and your horse can execute brilliantly and without any effort.

For the lower levels, this is pretty much the end of the warm-up. At higher levels, it would be at this point that a quick run-through of the difficult movements takes place: simple changes, flying changes, half-passes, pirouettes, and so on.

Most advanced horses need less time in the earlier stages after relaxation, in order to allow more time for the movements and transitions required in the latter part of warming-up. However, the total duration in most cases is still within the range of a half hour. Starting difficult movements too early in the warm-up only leads to evasion, resistance, tension and eventually, disobedience. This is exactly the opposite of what you want, but is a very frequent sight in the warm-up ring. It is much easier for a horse to give you all the difficult movements once he is warmed up than when you ask for them too early, when he is still stiff and not physically capable of executing them. Neither do you have to make a large number of these movements or transitions before you go to the ring, since if your horse cannot do them by now, he will not learn them at the show. If he knows them, he will only need a reminder.

Phase 4. Now, with the horse ready to perform, we are ready to proceed to the ring in a nice relaxed walk. As soon as you are allowed to enter the area around the ring, ride energetic, forward extensions, mediums, lengthenings and transitions that will convince your horse that he can do it on the new footing. Your own nervousness and tension will create all the collection you need once you enter at A. However, if you have not asked your horse and convinced him he can give you the maximum on the new footing, he will simply not be able to perform a perfect extension or medium trot during the first five movements, as is so often asked for right at the beginning of a test.

While riding by A, be absolutely sure where your line from A to C is located, whether to the right or left of the center of the opening of the gate, or if you are lucky, really in the middle. By the time the bell rings, you have done all you can, and you and your horse are ready to peak during the performance. You are not half dead, tense, exhausted and way below par, as many of your co-competitors will be. At this stage, physically speaking, after a sensible warm-up your horse's muscles are well supplied with oxygen and blood, warm, smoothly functioning, the energy reserves in the form of tracellular glucose have not been exhausted, nor has an oxygen deficiency developed, nor has there been any accumulation of waste products that could interfere ultimately with the performance. Adrenalin production is relatively high and the horse is mentally alert, feels good and ready to work. An indicator of the situation is that the horse is not yet in a real sweat, panting or looking tired.

If we consider the warm-up and the actual performance together, it is approximately 45 minutes of serious work. I consider this enough for every horse if the work has been concentrated and well organized.

I believe many horses get ring sour because they are totally depleted of reserves during the warm-up and then, with aching muscles and oxygen starved, are pushed into the ring and forced to perform. This is asking an unreasonable effort at the time when they are already totally exhausted and way beyond their physical performance peak. No wonder they hate the sight of the ring.

THE PSYCHCLOGICAL WARM-UP

The physiological warm-up is not all that counts. It must be coordinated with the psychological attitude of your horse. Warmbloods tend to be very easy as far as this is concerned. But the higher in blood they are and the younger, the more we must deal with psychological aspects. It is obviously dead wrong to ride a horse way over his physical peak, and to exhaust him psychologically, expecting a mentally and physically tired horse to perform miracles in the ring. Since the limitation is in the physical work schedule, we must deal with the psychological aspects of readiness separately if it does not fall within the time frame of our pre-planned physical warm-up.

With horses who have short attention spans, but are basically not high strung, long walk intervals maintain their psychological interest. Over-fit horses such as Thoroughbreds, and others with very high blood lines, have often a hard time settling down to work. The best warm-up plans can be ruined by such a situation. You must, therefore, deal with the psychological aspects separately by lungeing, or walking or riding the horse in a relaxed manner for as long as needed hours before the class. Ride quietly until he settles down, without any attempt at schooling. Then bring him back to the stable to relax with hay until the time to get ready for competition comes.

SOME FINAL TIPS

Here are a few reminders for when you get ready in your white britches and black boots:

First, make yourself a timetable and stick to it under all circumstances. Just because you are nervous is no justification to pull your horse out of the stall one hour early and grind him to a pulp.

If you have free time or don't know what to do, clean tack. Or, if you are a seasoned lady or an older gentleman, take a stirrup cup and relax. Depending on the number of rides, you may adjust the size of your tumbler! And, if your horse is an old hunter, remember hunting etiquette and offer him a snort, too.

Also, when competing, it is always the horse who is the star, not the competitor. So, turn him out the best you can and be conservative for yourself. Spare your bright makeup and jewelry for other occasions and don't force a smile if you don't really feel like it. Be neat, correct and conservative in your turn out.

Furthermore, remember that warming-up is not schooling, teaching, or trying something new. And, this is not the time to get into a fight with your horse. This is most likely caused by your own tenseness anyway, so don't blame this on him. Look at what you are doing and don't aggravate it further.

On a rainy day when there are big puddles in the ring and much splashing all over the place, wet down the legs and belly of your horse so he is less apprehensive of this fact. However, if your horse is an old hunter or has gone cross country through the water, he probably won't mind it at all.

Another helpful idea is to sew leather stops into the inside of your reins at, say, 26″, 30″, 34″, and 38″. This will allow you to be totally sure that the length of rein is the same throughout your performance. This can give you additional confidence and prevent slipping when wet.

This brings you up to the last few minutes and from then on in you are in the hands of the judge. Enjoy it! Do the best you can and you certainly won't be disappointed.

CHAPTER TWELVE

AFTER THE SHOW: EVALUATION

F O R all your trouble, expenses, and being dog-tired Monday morning at your job, why not get the most out of the test and not just a piece of paper or a ribbon? You can be proud to be fifth with a 66 percent ride, only to have been beaten by some Team and FEI riders showing their younger horses. On the other hand, getting a

Home from the show

blue ribbon with 58 percent must raise some questions over what went wrong.

So first ask yourself, was it a good test in the range of riding observed? Very often, competitors watch only Grand Prix or other advanced tests which may be very nice, but it would be better to watch the rides at approximately the same level as you are, especially those ridden by more experienced riders than you.

Recognizing the demands of the test, as well as your own difficulties, you may see while watching the more experienced riders hints of how to ride the transitions and movements. If in doubt, go and ask the rider how it was done. Dressage riding is not a secret science, and the better the rider, the more he or she will be happy to answer questions. These riders have all been there, too.

Dressage competitions are nothing but teaching and learning ex periences, and if you have mastered your lessons, keep a record of them.

Remember, as I said before, that movements and transitions up to Fourth Level are schooling exercises to prepare for bigger things and not an objective in themselves. Riding in competition and analyzing the scores afterwards always clarifies your weak and strong points in your schooling.

If you are serious about improving, make a chart as shown of the basic movements in your tests and enter the scores from each show. The results may be startling but, on close examination, it will be a valuable indication of what needs to be worked on. The chart shows very clearly the pattern of riding for our mythical competitor after the first three shows.

- We see that the entry, centerline, and halts are the pits, which also ruin the rein back. There is no excuse to have scores like this at Second Level if one has done the homework for technical movements properly the year before.

- The walk here is not the biggest movement but the most consistent. This rider should try not to push the horse too much so he starts jigging, or using too much rein, resulting in

CHART FOR A 2ND LEVEL HORSE

	1ST SHOW	2ND SHOW	3RD SHOW	4TH SHOW
ENTRY & CENTERLINE & HALT	4	5	5	
FINAL CENTERLINE & HALT	5	5	6	
HALTS	5	5	6	
BACKING	4	6	5	
WORKING WALK	6	6	6	
MEDIUM WALK	5	5	5	
TURN ON HAUNCHES LEFT	4	5	4	
TURN ON HAUNCHES RIGHT	7	6	6	
TRANSITION WALK-CANTER	4	5	7	
TRANSITION TROT-CANTER	7	6	7	
CANTER-WORKING	6	6	6	
CANTER-LENGTH	6	6	7	
CANTER-MEDIUM	5	5	6	
CANTER-CIRCLE RIGHT	7	7	6	
CANTER-CIRCLE LEFT	4	5	4	
CHANGE THROUGH TROT	6	6	6	
CHANGE SIMPLE R-L	4	4	5	
CHANGE SIMPLE L-R	6	6	7	
SHOULDER-IN LEFT	4	5	4	
SHOULDER-IN RIGHT	7	7	6	
TRAVERS LEFT	4	4	4	
TRAVERS RIGHT	7	6	7	
MEDIUM TROT	6	6	6	
COLLECTED TROT	5	6	6	
COUNTER CANTER RIGHT	6	6	7	
COUNTER CANTER LEFT	5	4	5	

pacing. Obviously not a strong point, but very little one can do about it.

■ The turn on the haunches to the left points to a basic deficiency in suppleness.

■ The canter work is basically coming along, except that the rider cannot ride a 10-meter circle to the left. This indicates the same basic lack of suppleness to the left.

■ The changes in canter through trot are about acceptable, but the simple changes to the left are poor and inadequate.

■ The shoulder-in and travers are lovely to the right, poor to the left, without bend or rhythm, and showing resistance. The trot circles are totally unacceptable to the left, and only borderline to the right.

Does this rider really need anything more to tell him what he should do now and what he should have done earlier? The lack of equal suppleness has hampered this rider throughout. It further shows that an omission in early training can cost dearly when trying to move up. The only way to make corrections is to go back and school the horse properly for equal suppleness before moving on confidently to Third, Fourth and higher levels, without any more problems in coping with a consistently weak side of the horse. I believe this approach is a good way to be honest with yourself and to get straightened out before it is too late. Another big question that arises here is how much of this problem is created by the rider rather than the horse. It's a good idea to have an expert look at what you're doing. Above all, don't blame your horse!

Charting test scores helps point out very early problems that ruin a test, and lets you know that mere repetition of the same movements is not the cure. The fundamental problem is something totally different, a flaw in basic training. Only you can correct it.

CHAPTER THIRTEEN:

A FEW THOUGHTS ON JUDGING

B Y now you have a good idea of what competitive dressage riding entails and a better appreciation of what is good and what is not so good when watching a performance in the ring. You also realize that awarding scores is not a matter of liking or not liking a certain movement, but that a judge has plenty of well-defined criteria to make an accurate assessment.

But, as we discussed earlier, judging only makes sense if the competitor understands the basic guidelines of the sport as defined by the AHSA, and can readily understand what the comments, suggestions, and scores actually mean. I hope this book will help you show your horse from his best side, to realize your shortcomings, and to understand why certain scores simply cannot be better unless you undertake to do something about them. They usually reflect a deficiency in basic training and it is important not to just gloss over a problem and drag it along from level to level, but to correct it as quickly as possible.

Since most judges have extensive showing and riding experience, one of their primary objectives is to point out what is good

in the ride, as well as the basic flaws, without being too heavily influenced by minor mistakes. For example, if a horse's trot lengthening on the diagonal loses the regularity of the rhythm for a few strides crossing the centerline at X, but regains it immediately, it is hardly worth noticing, particularly not at First Level. On the other hand, a horse rushing on the diagonal, coming off the bit and onto the forehand, and moving wide behind, even while lengthening the stride, is a serious matter and cannot be treated lightly.

Basically, judging should be rewarding the good, tempered by what is not correct and needs to be improved. Judging should not be just a "laundry list" of all the things that went wrong or could be better. If that were the case, anybody could sit at C and simply act as a fault-finder.

Judges make a major effort to be consistently fair and constructive. But, they are also human. Obviously, for you the competitor, the most important part of the twelve-hour day is the six or seven minutes you are in the ring. However, your score is only one in many. Judging is not as easy and often very demanding, physically and mentally, particularly if the show management imposes a schedule of a new horse every six minutes in the lower levels, which is impossible to keep.

In addition, every score from eight o'clock in the morning to six o'clock in the evening is posted and constitutes a permanent record open to criticism and comments during the show and later. Your own score is just one line on a long series of results. As a matter of fact, judges are much more on the spot than competitors. If they fail, one hundred competitors howl. If one competitor has poor results, nobody even notices.

Since the introduction of training courses for judges and an obligatory judges' forum, the uniformity and consistency of the officiating has greatly improved. There is a basic consensus of what is considered adequate or not adequate. Most judges, whether they agree or disagree with it, stick to this kind of a scale when officiating at recognized shows.

Now, while this book has given you some hints on how to compete better, good judging is much more complex. The key to

good judging is consistency, not only from 8:00 a.m. to 6:00 p.m., but show after show. This requires the judge to know and understand the test even better than you do, since every score incorporates a series of elements, the relative weight of which must be balanced. For instance, you see a good shoulder-in, but the rider does not straighten out before the corner. Obviously, an 8 is out of the question, but how much of an error is this? Or, in the canter depart at M the rider departs too soon, with haunches falling in and initially crooked on the long side, which he later desperately tries to correct. Is this belated correction good enough to make the movement sufficient? Or what about a centerline, where before C the rider swings out to the wrong side, but makes no other major mistakes. Can we reward a straight entry, good transition and halt by overlooking the sloppy riding after X? Certainly not. But how much do we assess this mistake?

Very often riders put horses into tests for which they are simply not yet ready, where the basic stages of training have not yet been mastered. This basic flaw, which shows up in every movement of the test, ruins the score, and can lead to some harsh comments of the judge. Take, for instance, a three-or four-year-old European Warmblood who looks like he's on the aids and who's put in a Second Level test. However, no matter how lovely he looks, he's not yet supple enough to both sides to ride correct 10-meter circles, shoulder-in, or travers. His insecurity and lack of balance shows clearly in his straddling in the lengthening, instead of a correct medium gait. Is there anything wrong with this lovely young horse who tries his best to do what is asked, but simply is not ready? Absolutely not. The mistake is with the rider or trainer who totally misunderstands that most of the basics have not yet been learned, no matter how nice a horse presents himself when looked at superficially.

A good judge, having seen almost anything you can imagine, has a pretty set system of judging. And not only that, very often when you judge a ride, you can almost predict what will happen. The judge knows exactly what he will be looking for in such cases. For instance, you can predict when you will likely see no

real transitions, leading to a faulty lengthening which will have to be scored at 4 or less.

So what does this mean for your own riding? Basically, even when riding only for one judge, try to ride as if there were five looking at you. Put in the most accuracy that you are capable of, but don't hesitate to use any of the suggestions you learned here to help you out of trouble and to support and maintain your horse. You can take a calculated risk at one point or another.

A good judge will always try to distinguish which mistakes are due to the rider and which are due to insufficient training of the horse. And in the lower levels, most mistakes are the rider's, not the horse's.

Remember, too, that most judges want to be constructive. They are trying to be helpful with their comments and scores, not simply documenting your failings as a rider. Try not to take them personally, but think of them as presenting you with a roadmap for your training. They really are not out to get you!

SHOW CHECKLIST

THE following list may be helpful to get you started on your own. If you forget something you can always borrow from a friend or your neighbor in the stable, as long as you return it with a nice "Thank you. "

PAPERS

❏ Copy of entry blanks
❏ Copy of time allotment from show secretary
❏ Test diagrams & AHSA test (USDF booklet)
❏ Copy of Coggins test
❏ Writing & felt markers
❏ AHSA *Rule Book*
❏ Stable card indicating horse's name, owner, hotel & telephone number
❏ Adhesive tape
❏ Copies of AHSA & USDF registration number for horse
❏ Copies of AHSA & USDF registration number for rider

SHIPPING OUTFIT

❑ Tail bandage
❑ 4 legwraps & 4 bandages
❑ Adhesive tape to secure bandages
❑ 4 bell boots to protect coronet bands (you can also use ready made shipping boots)
❑ Heavy duty leather halter & protective head cap (don't ship in nylon halters: they don't break in case of accident)
❑ Full hay net & carrots or tidbits
❑ 2 lead lines, one with a chain
❑ Lunge line for difficult loadings

TOOLS & HARDWARE

❑ Farrier tools if you know what to do if needed
❑ Hammer
❑ Pliers to cut wires & to remove nails from the stall
❑ Screwdrivers
❑ Drill
❑ Assorted size nails
❑ 16 eyescrews (various sizes) for feed bins, stall guards, etc.
❑ Tape & wire
❑ Stapler
❑ 12 snaps
❑ Rope

This all fits neatly in an old flight bag which should be the first item at hand when you arrive. Remember, the first chore is to fix the stall of your horse before unloading him.

STABLES

❑ Stable guards (2 depending on horse)
❑ Stall doors, metal frame or wire mesh & hinges if needed
❑ 2 water buckets
❑ 1 feed bucket

❑ 1 light leather or nylon halter
❑ 1 manure basket
❑ 2 manure forks
❑ 1 wheel barrel if space allows, with pail
❑ 1 broom
❑ Shavings enough for 2 full nights, minimum 4 bags
❑ Ant spray, particularly in the South
❑ Insect repellent
❑ Peppermint drops: if your horse refuses to drink water in a new stall, get him used to the peppermint flavor at home so he won't notice the difference at the show
❑ For stallions, plywood panels for stalls
❑ A length of rope
❑ Blanket
❑ Tack hook
❑ Saddle rack
❑ Removable hook for clothes hangers
❑ Flashlight

BLANKETS

❑ Fly sheet
❑ Rain sheet, as needed
❑ Cooler
❑ Lavenham
❑ Regular sheet or blanket, depending on season

COMFORT

❑ Folding chairs
❑ A cooler with cold drinks or hot coffee, depending on season

GROOMING

❑ Brushes
❑ Curry comb
❑ Towels

❏ Hoof dressing & hoof pick
❏ Braiding kit & milk crate to stand on
❏ Grooming spray, not on saddle areas—too slippery
❏ Fly spray
❏ Skin Bracer (Vetroline)
❏ Clipper or scissor set
❏ Wash bucket & sponges (don't mix up with feed & water
  buckets)
❏ Scraper
❏ Ivory soap liquid

MEDICAL SUPPLY

Be sure your horse has all vaccinations, tetanus, rhino, influenza,
encephalitis, etc.

❏ Telephone number of your vet at home
❏ Absorbine & polutice
❏ Wraps & bandages other than for shipping
❏ Disinfectant, local
❏ Antibiotic ointment
❏ Azium, in case of food or other allergies
❏ Rubbing alcohol, vetrolin bracer
❏ Cotton
❏ Gauze bandages
❏ Elastic bandages
❏ Thermometer
❏ Electrolytes
❏ Vitamins

TACK:

❏ Saddle
❏ 2 white girths
❏ 2 saddle pads, white or stable color (you use at least one set a
  day per horse)
❏ 2 pair reins: 1 leather for good weather, 1 canvas fabric or rubber for rain

❏ 1 whip, 4' or less (leave any whip longer than 4' at home, it could cause your elimination)

❏ Saddle soap & sponges

❏ Tack repair kit

❏ Swiss army knife

❏ Galloping boots

FEED:

❏ For one-day show, take your own drinking water for horse from home

❏ For washing down, use local supply

❏ Proper feed mix for sufficient feeding plus one extra meal for anticipated length of show

❏ Bran for cold or hot mash

❏ Electrolytes & vitamins

❏ Carrots & tidbits

❏ Hay, 2 times the normal amount for duration (horse cannot be turned out and should relax; cutting down feed a few days before show is good ideal)

CLOTHING (see also AHSA Rules)

For two day show:

❏ 2 white britches

❏ 2 white shirts *with* sleeves, short or long

❏ Choker

❏ Stockties, classical or velcro, 3 or 4

❏ Stock pins

❏ Black jacket in a clothes bag

❏ Cloth brush

❏ Spot remover

❏ Hunt cap

❏ Gloves: 1 with leather for good weather, 1 with rubber for rain, white or black

❏ Rain gear

❏ Overalls, blue jeans, wrap around skirt, etc., to protect white britches

❏ Sport jacket, rain proof (USET) type
❏ Show Boots
❏ Rubber boots
❏ Spurs, only if needed and the least aggressive possible
❏ Boot jack
❏ Boot hooks
❏ Powder for boots (to get on if wet)

MISCELLANEOUS

❏ Personal grooming kit & mirror—you must look just as neat,
   cool, fresh and collected as your horse
❏ Scratch paper & pen
❏ Combination lock for tack trunk to leave your valuables,
   jewelry or a few dollars you may want for refreshments

This list can obviously go on indefinitely and everybody has his
own ideas. however, if you go through this, you probably will
not forget too many of the essential items. Good luck and habe
a good show.

P.S. DON'T FORGET YOUR HORSE!

AHSA TESTS, TRAINING THROUGH SECOND LEVEL

TRAINING LEVEL TEST 1

NO.

Purpose: To confirm that the horse's muscles are supple and loose, and that it moves freely forward in a clear and steady rhythm, accepting contact with the bit. (Drawing shows movement #2)

Transitions in and out of the halt may be made through the walk.

Conditions:
Arena: Standard or small
Average time: 4:00
Maximum Possible Points: 220

	TEST	DIRECTIVE IDEAS	POINTS	COEFFICIENT	TOTAL	REMARKS
1. A	Enter working trot	Straightness on centerline,				
X	Halt, Salute	transitions, quality of halt				
	proceed working trot	and trot				
2. C	Track left	Quality of turn at C				
E	Circle left 20m	quality of trot, roundness				
		of circle				
3. Between						
K&A	Working canter left	Calmness and smoothness of				
	lead	depart				
4. A	Circle left 20m	Quality of canter, roundness				
		of circle				
5. Between						
B&M	Working trot	Balance during transition				
6. C	Medium walk	Transition, quality of walk				
7. HXF	Free walk	Straightness, quality of walk	2			
F	Medium walk					
8. A	Working trot	Smoothness of transition				
9. E	Circle right 20m	Quality of trot, roundness of				
		circle				
10. Between						
H&C	Working canter right	Calmness and smoothness of				
	lead	depart				
11. C	Circle right 20m	Quality of canter, roundness				
		of circle				
12. Between						
B&F	Working trot	Balance during transition				
13. A	Down centerline	Straightness on centerline,				
X	Halt, Salute	quality of trot and halt				

Leave arena at walk at A.

Sitting trot, rising trot or any combination thereof may be used when trot work is required

COLLECTIVE MARKS:

		POINTS		TOTAL	
Gaits (freedom and regularity)		2			
Impulsion (desire to move forward, elasticity of the steps, relaxation of the back)		2			
Submission (attention and confidence; harmony, lightness and ease of movements; acceptance of the bit)		2			
Rider's position and seat; correctness and effect of the aids		2			

FURTHER REMARKS:

SUBTOTAL   _____

ERRORS   (-_____)

TOTAL POINTS   _____

1995 TRAINING LEVEL TEST 2 | NO.

Purpose: To confirm that the horse's muscles are supple and loose, and that it moves freely forward in a clear and steady rhythm, accepting contact with the bit. (Drawing shows movement #13)

Transitions in and out of the halt may be made through the walk.

Conditions:
Arena: Standard or small
Average time: 4:30
Maximum Possible Points: 260

	TEST	DIRECTIVE IDEAS	POINTS	COEFFICIENT	TOTAL	REMARKS
1. A X	Enter working trot Halt, Salute Proceed working trot	Straightness on centerline, transitions, quality of halt and trot				
2. C M-B-F	Track right Straight ahead	Quality of turn at C, quality of trot, straightness				
3. A	Circle right 20m	Quality of trot, roundness of circle				
4. KXM	Change rein	Quality of trot, straightness				
5. C	Circle left 20m	Quality of trot, roundness of circle				
6. HXF	Change rein	Quality of trot, straightness				
7. A	Medium walk	Transition, quality of walk				
8. K-B B-M	Free walk Medium walk	Straightness, quality of walks, transitions	2			
9. M	Working trot	Balance during transition				
10. Between C&H	Working canter left lead	Calmness and smoothness of depart				
11. E	Circle left 20m	Quality of canter, roundness of circle				
12. Between E&K	Working trot	Smoothness of transition				
13. B E	Turn left Turn right	Quality of trot, quality of turns at B and E, straightness between turns				
14. Between C&M	Working canter right lead	Calmness and smoothness of depart,				
15. B	Circle right 20m	Quality of canter, roundness of circle				
16. Between B&F	Working trot	Smoothness of transition				
17. A X	Down centerline Halt, Salute	Straightness on centerline, quality of trot and halt				

Leave arena walk at A.
Sitting trot, rising trot or any combination thereof may be used when trot work is required

COLLECTIVE MARKS:

		POINTS	COEFFICIENT	TOTAL	
Gaits (freedom and regularity)			2		
Impulsion (desire to move forward, elasticity of the steps, relaxation of the back)			2		
Submission (attention and confidence; harmony, lightness and ease of movements; acceptance of the bit)			2		
Rider's position and seat; correctness and effect of the aids			2		

FURTHER REMARKS:

SUBTOTAL _____

ERRORS (-_____)

TOTAL POINTS _____

1995 TRAINING LEVEL TEST 3

NO.

Purpose: To confirm that the horse's muscles are supple and loose, and that it moves freely forward in a clear and steady rhythm, accepting contact with the bit. (Drawing shows movement #2/3)

Transitions in and out of the halt may be made through the walk.

Conditions:
Arena: Standard or small
Average time: 5:00
Maximum Possible Points: 260

		TEST	DIRECTIVE IDEAS	POINTS	COEFFICIENT	TOTAL	REMARKS
1.	A	Enter working trot sitting	Straightness on centerline, transitions,				
	X	Halt, Salute	quality of halt and trot				
		Proceed working trot sitting					
2.	C	Track left	Quality of turn at C, quality of				
	E	Turn left	trot and turn at E, roundness of				
	X	Circle left 20m	circle				
3.	X	Circle right 20m	Roundness of circle, quality of				
	B	Turn right	trot and turn at B				
4.	Between A&K	Working canter right lead	Calmness and smoothness of depart				
5.	E	Circle right 20m	Quality of canter, roundness of circle				
6.	Between E&H	Working trot sitting	Balance during transition				
7.	MXK	Change rein, working trot rising	Quality of trot, straightness				
	K	Working trot sitting					
8.	A	Medium walk	Transitions, quality of walk				
9.	FXM	Free walk	Straightness, quality of walks,	2			
	M	Medium walk	transitions				
10.	C	Working trot sitting	Quality of transition and trot				
11.	E	Circle left 20m, trot rising, letting the horse gradually take the reins out of the hands	Gradually giving and later taking the reins, horse stretching forward and downward with light contact while maintaining balance, rhythm and quality of trot	2			
	Before E	Gradually take up the reins					
	E	Working trot sitting and proceed straight ahead					
12.	Between A&F	Working canter left lead	Calmness and smoothness of depart				
13.	B	Circle left 20m	Quality of canter, roundness of circle				
14.	Between B&M	Working trot sitting	Balance during transition				
15.	HXF	Change rein, working trot rising	Quality of trot, straightness				
	F	Working trot sitting					
16.	A	Down centerline	Straightness on centerline,				
	X	Halt, Salute	quality of trot and halt				

Leave arena at walk at A.
All trot work sitting, unless otherwise indicated

COLLECTIVE MARKS:

Gaits (freedom and regularity)		2		
Impulsion (desire to move forward, elasticity of the steps, relaxation of the back)		2		
Submission (attention and confidence; harmony, lightness and ease of movements; acceptance of the bit)		2		
Rider's position and seat; correctness and effect of the aids		2		

FURTHER REMARKS:

SUBTOTAL _____

ERRORS   (-_____)

TOTAL POINTS _____

1995 TRAINING LEVEL TEST 4

NO.

Purpose: To confirm that the horse's muscles are supple and loose, and that it moves freely forward in a clear and steady rhythm, accepting contact with the bit. (Drawing shows movement #3)

Transitions in and out of the halt may be made through the walk.

Conditions:
Arena: Standard or small
Average time: 5:30
Maximum Possible Points: 250

		TEST	DIRECTIVE IDEAS	POINTS	COEFFICIENT	TOTAL	REMARKS
1.	A	Enter working trot sitting	Straightness on centerline,				
	X	Halt, Salute	transitions, quality of				
		proceed working trot sitting	halt and trot				
2.	C	Track right	Quality of turn at C, quality				
	B	Turn right	of trot, quality of turns				
	E	Turn left	at B and E, straightness between turns				
3.	FXM	One loop from F to X to M	Quality of trot, correctness of bending				
4.	Between C&H	Working canter left lead	Calmness and smoothness of depart				
5.	E	Circle left 20m	Quality of canter, roundness of circle				
6.	E	Working trot sitting and	Balance during transition, quality				
		proceed straight ahead	of trot				
7.	A-F-X	Medium Walk	Transition, quality of walk, straightness				
8.	X-H	Free walk	Straightness, quality of walks,	2			
	H	Medium walk	Transitions				
9.	C	Working trot sitting	Quality of transition and trot				
10.	B	Circle right 20m trot rising, letting the horse gradually take the reins out of the hands	Gradually giving and later taking the reins, horse stretching forward and downward with light contact, while maintaining balance, rhythm and quality of trot	2			
	Before B	Gradually take up the reins					
	B	Working trot sitting and proceed straight ahead					
11.	KXH	One loop from K to X to H	Quality of trot, correctness of bending				
12.	Between C&M	Working canter right lead	Calmness and smoothness of depart				
13.	B	Circle right 20m	Quality of canter, roundness of circle				
14.	B	Working trot sitting and proceed straight ahead	Balance during transition, quality of trot				
15.	A	Down centerline	Straightness on centerline,				
	X	Halt, Salute	quality of trot and halt				

Leave arena at walk at A.
All trot work sitting unless otherwise indicated

COLLECTIVE MARKS:

Gaits (freedom and regularity)	2		
Impusion (desire to move forward, elasticity of the steps, relaxation of the back)	2		
Submission (attention and confidence; harmony, lightness and ease of movements; acceptance of the bit)	2		
Rider's position and seat; correctness and effect of the aids	2		

FURTHER REMARKS:

SUBTOTAL   _____

ERRORS   (-_____)

TOTAL POINTS   _____

1995 FIRST LEVEL TEST 1

NO.

Purpose: To confirm that the horse, in addition to the requirements of Training Level, has developed thrust (pushing power) and achieved a degree of balance and throughness.(Diagram shows movement #5)

Conditions:
Arena: Standard or small
Average Time: 5:30
Maximum Possible Points: 280

		TEST	DIRECTIVE IDEAS	POINTS	COEFFICIENT ↓	TOTAL	REMARKS
1.	A X	Enter working trot Halt, Salute Proceed working trot	Straightness on centerline, transitions, quality of halt and trot				
2.	C E	Track left Half circle left 10m returning to the track at H	Quality of turn at C, quality of trot, execution and size of figure				
3.	B	Half circle right 10m returning to the track at M	Quality of trot, execution and size of figure				
4.	HXF F	Lengthen stride in trot rising Working trot sitting	Straightness, quality of trots and transitions				
5.	A-C	Serpentine of 3 equal loops width of arena	Quality of trot, execution of figure		2		
6.	C	Medium walk	Transition, quality of walk				
7.	MXF F	Free walk Medium walk	Straightness, quality of transitions		2		
8.	A	Working trot	Quality of transition and trot				
9.	K	Working canter right lead	Calmness and smoothness of depart				
10.	E	Circle right 15m	Quality of canter, roundness and size of circle				
11.	MXK X	Change rein Working trot	Straightness, balance during transition				
12.	F	Working canter left lead	Calmness and smoothness of depart				
13.	B	Circle left 15m	Quality of canter, roundness and size of circle				
14.	HXF X	Change rein Working trot	Straightness, balance during transition				
15.	A before A A	Circle right 20m working trot rising, letting the horse gradually take the reins out of the hands Take up the reins proceed ahead	Gradually giving and later taking the reins, horse stretching forward and downward with light contact, while maintaining balance, rhythm and quality of trot		2		
16.	KXM M	Lengthen stride in trot rising Working trot sitting	Straightness, quality of trots and transitions				
17.	E X G	Turn left Turn left Halt, Salute	Quality of trot, quality of turns at E and X, straightness on centerline, transition, quality of halt				

Leave arena at walk at A

COLLECTIVE MARKS:

		POINTS	COEFFICIENT	TOTAL	
	Gaits (freedom and regularity)		2		
	Impusion (desire to move forward, elasticity of the steps, relaxation of the back)		2		
	Submission (attention and confidence; harmony, lightness and ease of movements; acceptance of the bit)		2		
	Rider's position and seat; correctness and effect of the aids		2		

FURTHER REMARKS:

SUBTOTAL _____

ERRORS (-_____)

TOTAL POINTS _____

1995 FIRST LEVEL TEST 2

NO.

Purpose: To confirm that the horse, in addition to the requirements of Training Level, has developed thrust (pushing power) and achieved a degree of balance and throughness.(Diagram shows movement #3)

Conditions:
Arena: Standard or small
Average Time: 6:00
Maximum Possible Points: 310

		TEST	DIRECTIVE IDEAS	POINTS	COEFFICIENT	TOTAL	REMARKS
1.	A X	Enter working trot Halt, Salute Proceed working trot	Straightness on centerline, transitions, quality of halt and trot				
2.	C B E	Track right Turn right Turn left	Quality of turn at C, quality of trot, quality of turns at B and E, straightness between turns				
3.	A D-R	Down centerline Leg yield to the right (for small arena D-M)	Straightness on centerline, suppleness and alignment, quality of trot				
4.	C	Working canter left lead	Calmness and smoothness of depart				
5.	E	Circle left 15m	Quality of canter, roundness and size of circle				
6.	F-M	Lengthen stride in canter	Straightness, transition at F, quality of canter				
7.	M	Working canter	Balance during transition, quality of canter				
8.	HXF X	Change rein Working trot	Straightness, balance during transition				
9.	KXM M	Lengthen stride in trot rising Working trot sitting	Straightness, quality of trots and transitions		2		
10.	C	Halt 5 seconds Proceed medium walk	Quality of halt, transitions				
11.	HXF F	Free walk Medium walk	Straightness, quality of walks, transitions		2		
12.	A E B	Working trot Turn right Turn left	Quality of transition and trot, quality of turns at E and B, straightness between turns				
13.	HXF F	Lengthen stride in trot rising Working trot sitting	Straightness, quality of trots and transitions		2		
14.	A D-S	Down centerline Leg yield to the left (for small arena D-H)	Straightness on centerline, suppleness and alignment, quality of trot				
15.	C	Working canter right lead	Calmness and smoothness of depart				
16.	B	Circle right 15m	Quality of canter, roundness and size of circle				
17.	K-H	Lengthen stride in canter	Straightness, transition at K, quality of canter				
18.	H	Working canter	Balance during transition, quality of canter				
19.	MXK X	Change rein Working trot	Straightness, balance during transition				
20.	A X	Down centerline Halt, Salute	Straightness on centerline, quality of transition, and halt				

Leave arena at walk at A

COLLECTIVE MARKS:

Gaits (freedom and regularity)		2		
Impusion (desire to move forward, elasticity of the steps, relaxation of the back)		2		
Submission (attention and confidence; harmony, lightness and ease of movements; acceptance of the bit)		2		
Rider's position and seat; correctness and effect of the aids		2		

FURTHER REMARKS:

SUBTOTAL _____

ERRORS (-_____)

TOTAL POINTS _____

1995 FIRST LEVEL TEST 3

NO.

Purpose: To confirm that the horse, in addition to the requirements of Training Level, has developed thrust (pushing power) and achieved a degree of balance and throughness.(Diagram shows movements #2,3)

Conditions:
Arena: Standard
Average Time: 5:30
Maximum Possible Points: 350

		TEST	DIRECTIVE IDEAS	POINTS	COEFFICIENT ↓	TOTAL	REMARKS
1.	A X	Enter Working trot Halt, Salute Proceed working trot	Straightness on centerline, transitions, quality of halt and trot				
2.	C E-X	Track left Half circle left 10m	Quality of turn at C, quality of trot, execution and size of figure				
3.	X-B	Half circle right 10m	Quality of trot, execution and size of figure				
4.	V-I I	Leg yield to right Straight ahead	Quality of trot, suppleness and alignment, straightness on centerline	2			
5.	C MXK K	Track right Lengthen stride in trot rising Working trot sitting	Quality of turn at C, straightness, quality of trots, transitions				
6.	P-I I	Leg yield to the left Straight ahead	Quality of trot, suppleness and alignment, straightness on centerline	2			
7.	C HXF F	Track left Lengthen stride in trot sitting Working trot	Quality of turn at C, straightness, quality of trots, transitions				
8.	A	Halt, 5 seconds Proceed medium walk	Quality of halt, transitions				
9.	K-R R-M	Free Walk Medium Walk	Straightness, quality of walks, transitions	2			
10.	M C	Working trot Working canter left lead	Calmness and smoothness of transitions				
11.	S	Circle left 15m	Quality of canter,roundness and size of circle				
12.	S-K	Lengthen stride in canter	Transition at S, Straightness, quality of canter	2			
13.	K	Working canter	Balance during transition, quality of canter				
14.	FXH	Change rein, at X change of lead through trot	Straightness, calmness and smoothness of transitions				
15.	R	Circle right 15m	Quality of canter, roundness and size of circle				
16.	R-F	Lengthen stride in canter	Transition at R, straightness, quality of canter	2			
17.	F	Working canter	Balance during transition, quality of canter				
18.	KXM	Change rein, at X change of lead through trot	Straightness, calmness and smoothness of transitions				
19.	C	Working trot	Balance during transitions				
20.	E before E E	Circle left 20m trot rising, letting the horse gradually take the reins out of the hands Gradually take up the reins Working trot sitting	Gradually giving and later taking the reins, horse stretching forward and downward with light contact, while maintaining balance, rhythm and quality of trot	2			
21.	A X	Down Centerline Halt, Salute	Straightness on centerline, quality of trot and halt				

Leave arena at walk at A

COLLECTIVE MARKS:

Gaits (freedom and regularity)		2		
Impulsion (desire to move forward, elasticity of the steps, relaxation of the back)		2		
Submission (attention and confidence; harmony, lightness and ease of movements; acceptance of the bit)		2		
Rider's position and seat; correctness and effect of the aids		2		

FURTHER REMARKS:

SUBTOTAL _____

ERRORS   (-_____)

TOTAL POINTS _____

1995 FIRST LEVEL TEST 4

NO.

Purpose: To confirm that the horse, in addition to the requirements of Training Level, has developed thrust (pushing power) and achieved a degree of balance and throughness.(Diagram shows movement #3/4)

Conditions:
Arena: Standard
Average Time: 5:30
Maximum Possible Points: 330

COEFFICIENT

#		TEST	DIRECTIVE IDEAS	POINTS	COEFFICIENT	TOTAL	REMARKS
1.	A	Enter working trot	Straightness on centerline,				
	X	Halt, Salute	transitions, quality of				
		Proceed working trot	halt and trot				
2.	C	Track right	Quality of turn at C,		2		
	MXK	Lengthen stride in trot sitting	straightness, quality of				
	K	Working trot	trots, transitions				
3.	P	Circle left 10m	Quality of trot, roundness and				
	B	Turn left	size of circle, quality of				
			turn at B				
4.	E	Turn right	Quality of trot and turn at E,				
	S	Circle right 10m	roundness and size of circle				
5.	C	Halt 5 seconds	Quality of halt, transitions				
		Proceed medium walk					
6.	M-V	Free walk	Straightness, quality of		2		
	V	Medium walk	walks, transitions				
7.	K	Working trot	Calmness and smoothness				
	A	Working canter left lead	of transitions				
8.	F-M	Lengthen stride in canter	Transition at F, straightness,		2		
			quality of canter,				
9.	M	Working canter	Balance during transition,				
			quality of canter				
10.	C	Circle left 15m	Quality of canter, roundness				
			and size of circle				
11.	HXK	Single loop with no change of lead	Quality of canter, balance,				
			execution of figure				
12.	FXH	Change rein, at X,	Straightness, calmness and				
		change of lead through the trot	smoothness of transitions				
13.	M-F	Lengthen stride in canter	Transition at M, straightness,		2		
			quality of canter				
14.	F	Working canter	Balance during transition,				
			quality of canter				
15.	A	Circle right 15m	Quality of canter, roundness				
			and size of circle				
16.	KXH	Single loop with no change of lead	Quality of canter, balance,				
			execution of figure				
17.	MXK	Change rein at X	Straightness, calmness and				
		change of lead through trot	smoothness of transitions				
18.	A	Working trot	Balance during transition				
19.	FXH	Lengthen stride in trot sitting	Straightness, quality of		2		
	H	Working trot	trots, transitions				
20.	B	Turn right	Quality of trot, straightness				
	X	Turn right	on centerline, quality of				
	G	Halt, Salute	turns, halt, transition				

Leave arena at walk at A

COLLECTIVE MARKS:

Gaits (freedom and regularity)		2		
Impusion (desire to move forward, elasticity of the steps, relaxation of the back)		2		
Submission (attention and confidence; harmony, lightness and ease of movements; acceptance of the bit)		2		
Rider's position and seat; correctness and effect of the aids		2		

FURTHER REMARKS:

SUBTOTAL _____

ERRORS   (-_____)

TOTAL POINTS _____

1995 SECOND LEVEL TEST 1

NO. [_____]

Purpose: To confirm that the horse, having demonstrated that it has achieved the thrust (pushing power) required in First Level, now shows that through additional training it accepts more weight on the hind quarters (collection). shows the thrust required at medium paces and is reliably on the bit. A greater degree of straightness, bending, suppleness. throughness and self-carriage is required than at First Level. (Diagram shows movement #15)

Conditions:
Arena: Standard
Average time: 6:30
Maximum possible points: 390

		TEST	DIRECTIVE IDEAS	POINTS	COEFFICIENT	TOTAL	REMARKS
1.	A / X	Enter collected trot / Halt, Salute / Proceed collected trot	Straightness on centerline, transitions, quality of halt and trot				
2.	C / HXF / F	Track left / Medium trot / Collected Trot	Quality of turn at C, straightness, quality of trots				
3.		The Transitions at H and F	Balance during transitions				
4.	V	Circle right 10m	Quality of trot, roundness and size of circle				
5.	V-S	Shoulder-in right	Quality of trot, execution of movement		2		
6.	MXK / K	Medium trot / Collected trot	Straightness, quality of trots				
7.		The Transitions at M and K	Balance during transitions				
8.	P	Circle Left 10m	Quality of trot, roundness and size of circle				
9.	P-R	Shoulder-in left	Quality of trot, execution of movement		2		
10.	C	Halt, reinback 3-4 steps proceed medium walk	Quality of halt and rein back, transitions				
11.	HXF / F	Free walk / Medium walk	Straightness, quality of walks, transitions		2		
12.	Before A / A	Shorten the stride / Collected canter right lead	Calmness and smoothness of depart				
13.	S-I / IKA	Half circle right 10m to centerline / Change rein no change of lead	Execution and size of figure, quality of canter and counter canter, straightness				
14.	AFP / PH	Proceed in counter canter / Change rein	Quality of canter and counter canter, straightness				
15.	C	Circle right 20m, upon crossing centerline, rider extends inside hand forward, up the horse's neck for 3-4 strides, maintaining contact on the outside rein	Clear release of contact where the horse maintains self-carriage, rhythm, bend and quality of canter		2		
16.	M-F / F	Medium canter / Collected canter	Straightness, quality of canters				
17.		The transitions at M and F	Balance during transitions				
18.	KXM	Change rein, at X change of lead through trot	Straightness, calmness and smoothness of transitions				
19.	C	Circle left 20m, upon crossing centerline, rider extends inside hand forward, up the horse's neck for 3-4 strides, maintaining contact on the outside rein	Clear release of contact where the horse maintains self-carriage, rhythm, bend and quality of canter		2		
20.	V-L / LHC	Half circle left 10m to centerline / Change rein, no change of lead	Execution and size of figure, quality of canter and counter canter, straightness				
21.	CMR / R-K	Proceed in counter canter / Change rein	Quality of canter and counter canter, straightness				
22.	F-M / M	Medium Canter / Collected Canter	Straightness, quality of canter				
23.		The Transitions at F and M	Balance during transitions				
24.	HXF	Change rein, at X change of lead through trot	Straightness, calmness and smoothness of transitions				
25.	F	Collected trot	Balance during transition				
26.	A / X	Down Centerline / Halt, Salute	Straightness on centerline, quality of trot, transition and halt				

Leave arena at walk at A

COLLECTIVE MARKS:

	POINTS	COEFFICIENT	TOTAL	REMARKS
Gaits (freedom and regularity)		2		
Impulsion (desire to move forward, elasticity of the steps, suppleness of the back and engagement of the hindquarters)		2		
Submission (attention and confidence; harmony, lightness and ease of movements; acceptance of the bridle and lightness of the forehand)		2		
Rider's position and seat; correctness and effect of the aids		2		

FURTHER REMARKS:

SUBTOTAL [_____]

ERRORS (- [_____])

TOTAL POINTS [_____]

Reprinted with permission of AHSA. © 1994 American Horse Show Association, Inc. All rights reserved. Reproduction without permission prohibited by law.

1995 SECOND LEVEL TEST 2

NO. _____

Purpose: To confirm that the horse, having demonstrated that it has achieved the thrust (pushing power) required in First Level, now shows that through additional training it accepts more weight on the hind quarters (collection), shows the thrust required at medium paces and is reliably on the bit. A greater degree of straightness, bending, suppleness, throughness and self-carriage is required than at First Level. (Diagram shows movements #2/3)

Conditions:
Arena: Standard
Average time: 6:00
Maximum possible points: 380

		TEST	DIRECTIVE IDEAS	POINTS	COEFFICIENT	TOTAL	REMARKS
1.	A X	Enter collected trot Halt, Salute Proceed collected trot	Straightness on centerline, transitions, quality of halt and trot				
2.	C M-B	Track right Shoulder-in right	Quality of turn at C, quality of trot, execution of movement				
3.	B	Circle right 10m	Quality of trot, roundness and size of circle				
4.	KXM M	Medium trot Collected trot	Straightness, quality of trots		2		
5.		Transitions at K and M	Balance during transitions				
6.	H-E	Shoulder-in left	Quality of trot, execution of movement				
7.	E	Circle left 10m	Quality of trot, roundness and size of circle				
8.	FXH H	Medium trot Collected trot	Straightness, quality of trots		2		
9.		Transitions at F and H	Balance during transition				
10.	C	Halt, reinback 3-4 steps Proceed medium walk	Quality of halt and rein back, transitions				
11.	MXK K	Free walk Medium walk	Straightness, quality of walks, transitions		2		
12.	Before A A	Shorten the stride Collected canter left lead	Calmness and smoothness of depart				
13.	A-C	Serpentine of 3 equal loops width of arena, no change of lead	Quality of canter and counter canter, execution of figure		2		
14.	C	Circle left 10m	Quality of canter, roundness and size of circle				
15	H-K K	Medium canter Collected canter	Straightness, quality of canter		2		
16.		The Transitions at H and K	Balance during transitions				
17.	FXH	Change rein, at X change of lead through the trot	Straightness, calmness and smoothness of transitions				
18.	C-A	Serpentine of 3 equal loops width of arena, no change of lead	Quality of canter and counter canter, execution of figure		2		
19.	A	Circle right 10m	Quality of canter, roundness and size of circle				
20.	K-H H	Medium canter Collected canter	Straightness, quality of canter		2		
21.		The Transitions at K and H	Balance during transitions				
22.	MXK	Change of rein, at X change of lead through the trot	Straightness, calmness and smoothness of transitions				
23.	A L G	Down centerline Collected trot Halt, Salute	Straightness on centerline, Quality of trot and halt, Transitions				

Leave arena at walk at A

COLLECTIVE MARKS:

	POINTS	COEFFICIENT	TOTAL	
Gaits (freedom and regularity)		2		
Impulsion (desire to move forward, elasticity of the steps, suppleness of the back and engagement of the hind quarters)		2		
Submission (attention and confidence; harmony, lightness and ease of movements; acceptance of the bridle and lightness of the forehand)		2		
Rider's position and seat; correctness and effect of the aids		2		

FURTHER REMARKS:

SUBTOTAL _____

ERRORS (-_____)

TOTAL POINTS _____

1995 SECOND LEVEL TEST 3 | NO.

Purpose: To confirm that the horse, having demonstrated that it has achieved the thrust (pushing power) required in First Level, now shows that through additional training it accepts more weight on the hind quarters (collection), shows the thrust required at medium paces and is reliably on the bit. A greater degree of straightness, bending, suppleness, throughness and self-carriage is required than at First Level. (Diagram shows movements #5/6)

Conditions:
Arena: Standard
Average time: 6:00
Maximum possible points: 430

		TEST	DIRECTIVE IDEAS	POINTS	COEFFICIENT	TOTAL	REMARKS
1.	A	Enter collected trot	Straightness on centerline				
	X	Halt, salute	transitions, quality of halt				
		Proceed collected trot	and trot				
2.	C	Track left	Quality of turn at C, quality of				
	H-E	Shoulder-in left	trot, execution of the movement				
3.	E-X	Half circle left 10m	Quality of trot, roundness and				
	X-B	Half circle right 10m	size of figure				
4.	B-F	Shoulder in right	Quality of trot, execution of the movement				
5.	V	Circle right 10m	Quality of trot, roundness and size of circle				
6.	V-S	Travers right	Quality of trot, execution of movement	2			
7.	MXK	Medium trot	Straightness, quality of trots				
	K	Collected trot					
8.		Transitions at M and K	Balance during transitions				
9.	P	Circle left 10m	Quality of trot, roundness and size of circle				
10.	P-R	Travers left	Quality of trot, execution of movement	2			
11.	HXF	Medium trot	Straightness, quality of trots				
	F	Collected trot					
12.		Transitions at H and F	Balance during transitions				
13.	A	Halt, reinback 3 or 4 steps proceed medium walk	Quality of halt and reinback, transitions				
14.	KXM	Free walk	Straightness, quality of free walk	2			
	M	Medium walk	transitions				
15.	Between H&S	Shorten the stride and half turn on the haunches left, proceed medium walk	Execution of movement				
16.	Between M&R	Shorten the stride and half turn on the haunches right, proceed medium walk	Execution of movement				
17.		The Medium walk AKXMCH(S)HCM(R)M	Quality of walk				
18.	Before C	Shorten the stride	Calmness and smoothness of depart				
	C	Collected canter left lead					
19.	E	Circle left 10m	Quality of canter, roundness and size of circle				
20.	Between E&V	Simple change of lead	Calmness and smoothness of change				
21.	VKAF	Counter canter	Quality of counter canter and canter,	2			
	F-S	Change rein	straightness				
22.	M-F	Medium canter	Straightness, quality of canters				
	F	Collected canter					
23.		Transitions at M and F	Balance during transitions				
24.	E	Circle right 10m	Quality of canter, roundness and size of circle				
25.	Between E&S	Simple change of lead	Calmness and smoothness of change				
26.	SHCM	Counter canter	Quality of counter canter and	2			
	MV	Change rein	canter, straightness				
27.	F-M	Medium canter	Straightness, quality of canters				
	M	Collected canter					
28.		Transitions at F and M	Balance during transitions				
29.	C	Collected trot	Balance during transition				
30.	E	Turn left	Quality of turns at E and X,				
	X	Turn left	quality of trot and halt,				
	G	Halt, Salute	transition				

Leave arena at walk at A

COLLECTIVE MARKS:

	POINTS	COEFFICIENT	TOTAL	REMARKS
Gaits (freedom and regularity)		2		
Impulsion (desire to move forward, elasticity of the steps, suppleness of the back and engagement of the hindquarters)		2		
Submission (attention and confidence; harmony, lightness and ease of movements; acceptance of the bridle and lightness of the forehand)		2		
Rider's position and seat; correctness and effect of the aids		2		

FURTHER REMARKS:

SUBTOTAL _____

ERRORS (- _____)

TOTAL POINTS _____

1995 SECOND LEVEL TEST 4

	NO.

Purpose: To confirm that the horse, having demonstrated that it has achieved the thrust (pushing power) required in First Level, now shows that through additional training it accepts more weight on the hind quarters (collection), shows the thrust required at medium paces and is reliably on the bit. A greater degree of straightness, bending, suppleness, throughness and self-carriage is required than at First Level. (Diagram shows movement#20)

Conditions:
Arena: Standard
Average time: 6:30
Maximum possible points: 440

COEFFICIENT

		TEST	DIRECTIVE IDEAS	POINTS	÷	TOTAL	REMARKS
1.	A	Enter collected trot	Straightness on centerline.				
	X	Halt, Salute	transitions, quality of halt and trot				
		proceed collected trot					
2.	C	Track right	Quality of turn at C.		2		
	MXK	Medium trot	quality of trots,				
	K	Collected trot	straightness				
3.		The Transitions at M and K	Balance during transitions				
4.	F-B	Shoulder-in left	Quality of trot, execution of movement				
5.	B	Circle left 10m	Quality of trot, roundness and size of circle				
6.	B-M	Travers left	Quality of trot, execution of movement				
7.	HXF	Medium trot	Quality of trots, straightness		2		
	F	Collected trot					
8.		The Transitions at H and F	Balance during transitions				
9.	K-E	Shoulder-in right	Quality of trot, execution of movement				
10.	E	Circle right 10m	Quality of trot, roundness and size of circle				
11.	E-H	Travers right	Quality of trot, execution of movement				
12.	C	Halt, reinback 3 or 4 steps	Quality of halt and reinback, transitions				
		proceed medium walk					
13.	M	Turn right					
	Between						
	G&H	Shorten the stride and half turn on the haunches right proceed medium walk	Execution of movement				
14.	Between						
	G&M	Shorten the stride and half turn on the haunches left Proceed medium walk	Execution of movement				
	H	Turn left					
15.		The Medium walk CMG(H)G(M)GHS	Quality of walk				
16.	S-F	Free walk	Straightness, quality of walk,		2		
	F	Medium walk	transitions				
17.	Before						
	A	Shorten stride in the walk	Calmness and smoothness of depart				
	A	Collected canter right lead					
18.	V	Circle right 10m	Quality of canter, roundness and size of circle				
19.	E	Simple change of lead	Calmness and smoothness of change		2		
20.	S-R	Half circle right 20m in counter canter	Quality of canter and counter canter, straightness				
	R-K	Change rein					
21.	P	Circle left 10m	Quality of canter, roundness and size of circle				
22.	B	Simple change of lead	Calmness and smoothness of change		2		
23.	R-S	Half circle left 20m in counter canter	Quality of canter and counter canter, straightness				
	S-F	Change rein					
24.	K-H	Medium canter	Quality of canters, straightness		2		
	H	Collected canter					
25.		Transitions at K and H	Balance during transitions				
26.	B	Turn right	Quality of canter, quality of turns at B and E, calmness and smoothness change				
	X	Simple change of lead					
	E	Turn left					
27.	F-M	Medium canter	Straightness, quality of canters		2		
	M	Collected canter					
28.		The transitions at F and M	Balance during transitions				
29.	S	Collected trot	Balance during transition, quality of trot, turns and halt				
	E	Turn left					
	X	Turn left					
	G	Halt, Salute					

Leave arena at walk at A

COLLECTIVE MARKS:

Gaits (freedom and regularity)	2	
Impusion (desire to move forward, elasticity of the steps, suppleness of the back and engagement of the hindquarters)	2	
Submission (attention and confidence; harmony, lightness and ease of movements; acceptance of the bridle and lightness of the forehand)	2	
Rider's position and seat; correctness and effect of the aids	2	

FURTHER REMARKS:

SUBTOTAL _____
ERRORS (- _____)
TOTAL POINTS _____